**AUTHORS**

ELAINE MEI AOKI
VIRGINIA A. ARNOLD
JAMES FLOOD
JAMES V. HOFFMAN
DIANE LAPP
MIRIAM MARTINEZ
ANNEMARIE SULLIVAN PALINCSAR
MICHAEL PRIESTLEY
NANCY ROSER
CARL B. SMITH
WILLIAM H. TEALE
JOSEFINA VILLAMIL TINAJERO
ARNOLD W. WEBB
PEGGY E. WILLIAMS
KAREN D. WOOD



**MACMILLAN/McGRAW-HILL SCHOOL PUBLISHING COMPANY**

**NEW YORK CHICAGO COLUMBUS**

# AUTHORS, CONSULTANTS, AND REVIEWERS

## WRITE IDEA! Authors

Elaine Mei Aoki, James Flood, James V. Hoffman, Diane Lapp, Ana Huerta Macias, Miriam Martinez, Ann McCallum, Michael Priestley, Nancy Roser, Carl B. Smith, William Strong, William H. Teale, Charles Temple, Josefina Villamil Tinajero, Arnold W. Webb, Peggy E. Williams

The approach to writing in Macmillan/McGraw-Hill Reading/Language Arts is based on the strategies and approaches to composition and conventions of language in Macmillan/McGraw-Hill's writing-centered language arts program, WRITE IDEA!

## Multicultural and Educational Consultants

Alma Flor Ada, Yvonne Beamer, Joyce Buckner, Helen Gillotte, Cheryl Hudson, Narcita Medina, Lorraine Monroe, James R. Murphy, Sylvia Peña, Joseph B. Rubin, Ramon Santiago, Cliff Trafzer, Hai Tran, Esther Lee Yao

## Literature Consultants

Ashley Bryan, Joan I. Glazer, Paul Janeczko, Margaret H. Lippert

## International Consultants

Edward B. Adams, Barbara Johnson, Raymond L. Marshall

## Music and Audio Consultants

John Farrell, Marilyn C. Davidson, Vincent Lawrence, Sarah Pirtle, Susan R. Snyder, Rick and Deborah Witkowski

## Teacher Reviewers

Terry Baker, Jane Bauer, James Bedi, Nora Bickel, Vernell Bowen, Donald Cason, Jean Chaney, Carolyn Clark, Alan Cox, Kathryn DesCarpentrie, Carol L. Ellis, Roberta Gale, Brenda Huffman, Erma Inscore, Sharon Kidwell, Elizabeth Love, Isabel Marcus, Elaine McCraney, Michelle Moraros, Earlene Parr, Dr. Richard Potts, Jeanette Pulliam, Michael Rubin, Henrietta Sakamaki, Kathleen Cultron Sanders, Belinda Snow, Dr. Jayne Steubing, Margaret Mary Sulentic, Barbara Tate, Seretta Vincent, Willard Waite, Barbara Wilson, Veronica York

# ACKNOWLEDGMENTS

*The publisher gratefully acknowledges permission to reprint the following copyrighted material:*

"Amelia Bedelia's Family Album" is excerpted from AMELIA BEDELIA'S FAMILY ALBUM by Peggy Parish with illustrations by Lynn Sweat. Text copyright © 1988 by Peggy Parish. Illustrations copyright © 1988 by Lynn Sweat. Published by Greenwillow Books and reprinted by permission of William Morrow and Compnay, Inc., Publishers, New York.

The book cover of CAN I KEEP HIM?: From CAN I KEEP HIM? by Steven Kellogg. Copyright © 1971 by Steven Kellogg. Used by permission of Dial Books for Young Readers, a division of Penguin Books USA Inc.

"Carry Go Bring Come." From CARRY GO BRING COME by Vyanne Samuels. Copyright © 1988 by Vyanne Samuels. Illustrations copyright © 1988 by Jennifer Northway. Reprinted with permission from Four Winds Press, an imprint of Macmillan Publishing Company. Reprinted also by permission of the Bodley Head.

"Eletelephony" from TIRRA LIRRA RHYMES OLD AND NEW by Laura Richards. Copyright 1930 by Laura Richards. Copyright renewed 1960 by Hamilton Richards. Printed by permission of Little, Brown and Company.

"Everybody says" from EVERYTHING AND ANYTHING by Dorothy Aldis. Copyright 1925-1927, copyright renewed © 1953-1955 by Dorothy Aldis. Reprinted by permission of G.P. Putnam's Sons.

"Family Pictures." from the book FAMILY PICTURES by Carmen Lomas Garza. Copyright © 1990 by Carmen Lomas Garza. Reprinted by permission of GRM Associates, Inc., Agents for Children's Book Press. Self-portrait of the author is copyright © 1990 by Carmen Lomas Garza and also is reprinted by permission of GRM Associates, Inc., Agents for Children's Book Press.

The book cover of FLY AWAY HOME by Eve Bunting, illustrated by Ronald Himler, Copyright © 1991, published by Clarion Books of Houghton Mifflin, is reprinted by permission of the publisher.

"The Goat in the Rug." From THE GOAT IN THE RUG by Charles Blood and Martin Link. Copyright © 1980 by Charles L. Blood and Martin A. Link. Illustrations copyright © 1980 by Nancy Winslow Parker. Reprinted with permission from Four, Winds Press, an imprint of Macmillan Publishing Company.

The book cover of HENRY AND MUDGE AND THE FOREVER SEA by Cynthia Rylant, illustrated by Suçie Stevenson. Copyright for the illustration 1989 by Suçie Stevenson. Reprinted by permission of Bradbury Press, an affiliate of Macmillan, Inc.

"Henry and Mudge: The First Book." Text by Cynthia Rylant, illustrations by Suçie Stevenson. Text copyright © 1987 by Cynthia Rylant. Illustrations copyright © 1987 by Suçie Stevenson. Reprinted with permission of Bradbury Press, an affiliate of Macmillan, Inc.

"Henry's Wrong Turn." From HENRY'S WRONG TURN by Harriet Ziefert with illustrations by Andrea Baruffi. Text copyright © 1989 by Harriet Ziefert. Illustrations copyright © 1989 by Andrea Barufi. By permission of Little, Brown and Company.

"Hugs and Kisses" from THE SUN IS ON by Lindamichellebaron. Reprinted by permission of Harlin Jacque Publications.

The book cover of THE ISLAND OF THE SKOG: From THE ISLAND OF THE SKOG by Steven Kellogg. Copyright © 1973 by Steven Kellogg. Used by permission of Dial Books for Young Readers, a division of Penguin Books USA Inc.

"K" (A kettle's for the kitchen) is from CERTAINLY, CARRIE CUT THE CAKE by Margaret and John Travers Moore. Copyright © 1971 by Margaret and John Travers Moore, published by the Bobbs-Merrille Co. Reprinted by permission of John Travers Moore.

"The Light-House-Keeper's White-Mouse" from YOU READ TO ME, I'LL READ TO YOU by John Ciardi. Copyright © 1962 by John Ciardi. Copyright © 1990 renewed. Reprinted by permission of Mrs. Judith Ciardi.

*(Continued on page 367)*



Macmillan/McGraw-Hill School Division
10 Union Square East
New York, New York 10003

Printed in the United States of America
ISBN 0-02-178756-5 / 2, L.6
3 4 5 6 7 8 9 RAI 99 98 97 96 95 94 93

DEDICATION FROM THE DEVELOPMENT TEAM. . .

*To Marjorie Dennison:*

*My second grade teacher and the first person to make reading and writing come alive for me.*

*Cynthia Chapman*

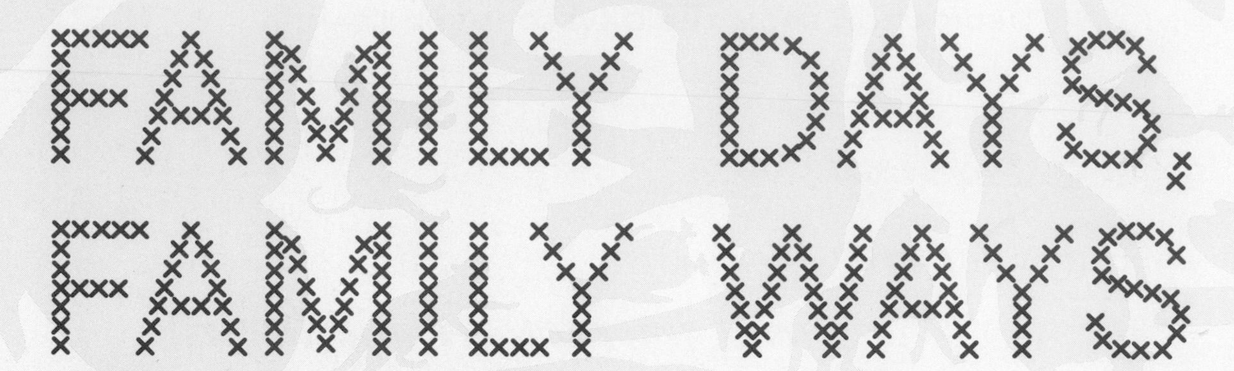
FAMILY DAYS,
FAMILY WAYS

### *Poetry*



### *More to Explore*



### *Books from the Classroom Library*

UNIT 2

# NOW I Know!

# TEAMING UP

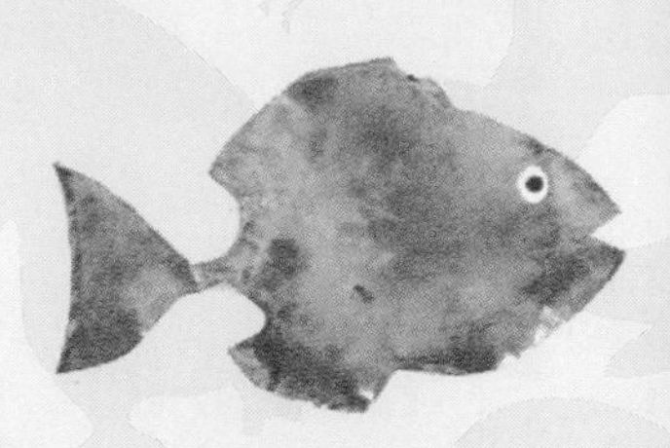

256
## The Goat in the Rug

A social studies story
*written by Charles L. Blood and Martin Link, illustrated by Nancy Winslow Parker*
**New York Times Best Illustrated Children's Books of the Year Award–winning illustrator**

**Notable Children's Trade Book in the Field of Social Studies, 1976; Children's Study Association Children's Book of the Year, 1976**

Geraldine the goat tells this story of cooperation in which she and Glenmae, a Navajo weaver, follow the step-by-step process of turning Geraldine's wool into a beautiful Navajo rug.

224
## The Mysterious Tadpole

A fantasy
*written and illustrated by Steven Kellogg*
**Art Books for Children and New York Times Best Illustrated Children's Books of the Year Award–winning illustrator**

**Irma Simonton Black Award, 1977; ALA Notable Book for Children, 1977; Children's Book Council Classroom Choice, 1977**

When is a tadpole not really a tadpole? Steven Kellogg answers this question in his imaginative story about a friendship between a young boy name Louis and his not-so-ordinary tadpole, Alphonse.

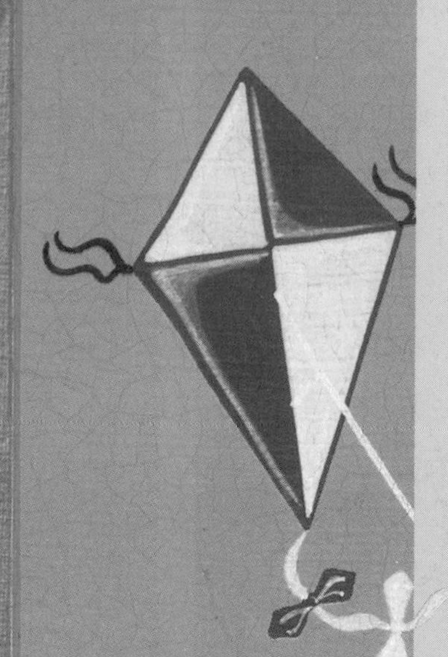

# CONTENTS

UNIT

1

# Family Days, Family Ways

We're all a family
Under one sky
We're a family under one sky.

from a song by
RUTH PELHAM

## Meet Cynthia Rylant

Cynthia Rylant says, "The idea for Henry and Mudge came from my own life. I once owned a 200-pound English mastiff named Mudge. My son, Nate, was seven years old at the time. The two together became Henry and Mudge in my books.

"Anyone who's ever loved a dog knows what a treasure a good dog is. You just can't be unhappy for very long when you have a good dog licking your face, shaking your hand, and drooling all over your shoes."

## Meet Suçie Stevenson

Suçie Stevenson loves to draw pictures for the stories about Henry and Mudge. She says: "The stories are about things that have happened to me."

When asked if she had anything to tell children who might like to be artists, Ms. Stevenson said: "Don't listen to what others tell you to draw. Put colors where you want them. Just start drawing."

# Henry and Mudge

Story by Cynthia Rylant
Pictures by Suçie Stevenson

## Henry

Henry had no brothers
and no sisters.
"I want a brother,"
he told his parents.
"Sorry," they said.
Henry had no friends
on his street.

"I want to live
on a different street,"
he told his parents.
"Sorry," they said.
Henry had no pets
at home.
"I want to have a dog,"
he told his parents.
"Sorry," they *almost* said.

But first they looked
at their house
with no brothers and sisters.
Then they looked
at their street
with no children.
Then they looked
at Henry's face.

Then they looked at each other.
“Okay,” they said.
“I want to hug you!”
Henry told his parents.
And he did.

# Mudge

Henry searched for a dog.

"Not just any dog," said Henry.

"Not a short one," he said.

"Not a curly one," he said.

"And no pointed ears."

Then he found Mudge.
Mudge had floppy ears,
not pointed.
And Mudge had straight fur,
not curly.
But Mudge was short.
"Because he's a puppy,"
Henry said.
"He'll grow."

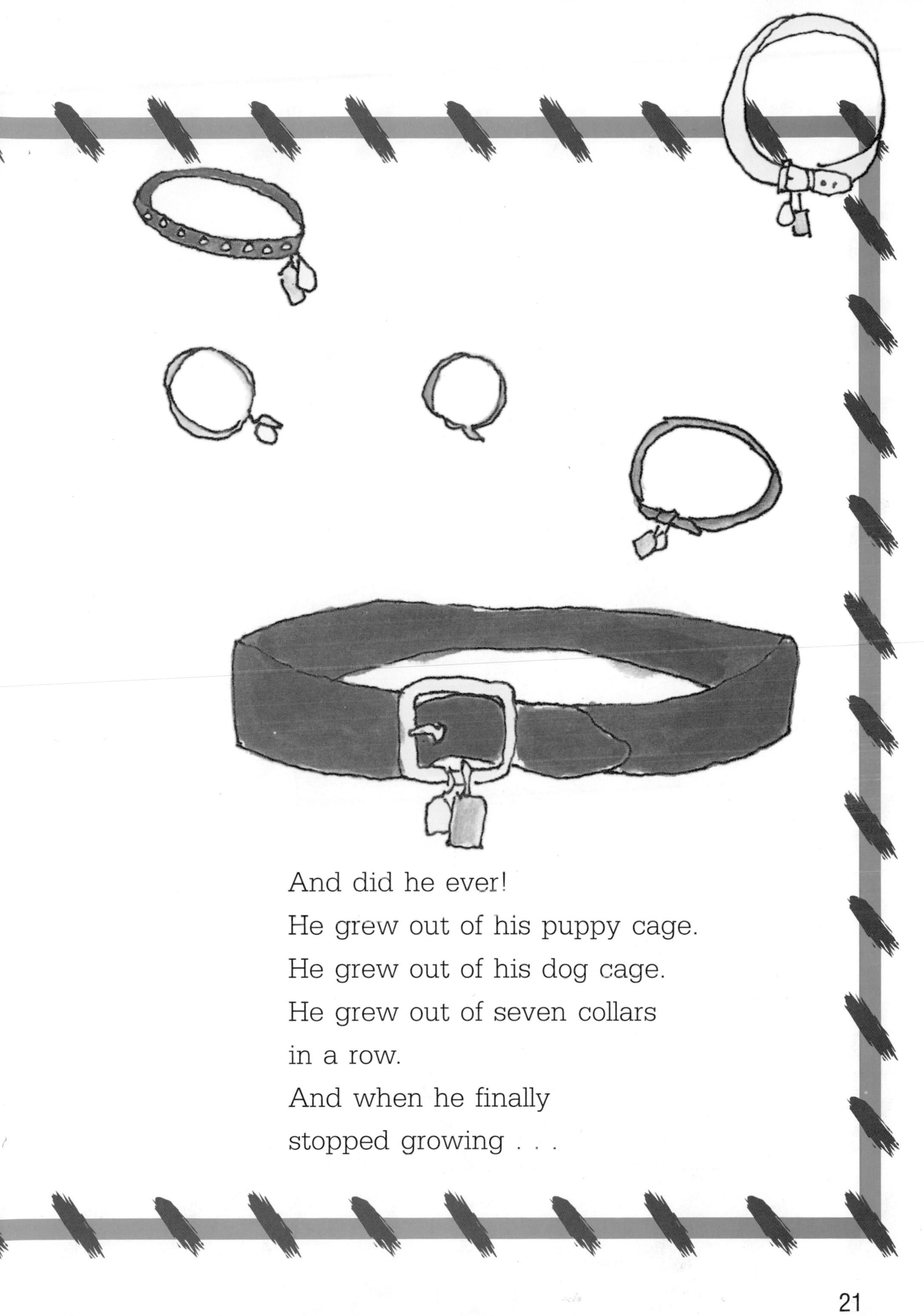

And did he ever!
He grew out of his puppy cage.
He grew out of his dog cage.
He grew out of seven collars
in a row.
And when he finally
stopped growing . . .

he weighed one hundred eighty pounds,
he stood three feet tall,
and he drooled.
"I'm glad you're not short,"
Henry said.

And Mudge licked him,
then sat on him.

# Henry

Henry used to walk
to school alone.
When he walked
he used to worry about
tornadoes,
ghosts,
biting dogs,
and bullies.

He walked as fast
as he could.
He looked straight ahead.
He never looked back.
But now he walked to school
with Mudge.

And now when he walked,
he thought about
vanilla ice cream,
rain,
rocks,
and good dreams.
He walked to school
but not too fast.
He walked to school
and sometimes backward.

He walked to school
and patted Mudge's big head,
happy.

# October Saturday

by Bobbi Katz

All the leaves have turned to cornflakes.
It looks as if some giant's baby brother
had tipped the box
and scattered them upon our lawn—
millions and millions of cornflakes—
crunching, crunching under our feet.
When the wind blows,
they rattle against each other,
nervously chattering.

We rake them into piles—
Dad and I.
Piles and piles of cornflakes!
A breakfast for a whole family of giants!
We do not talk much as we rake—
a word here—
a word there.
The leaves are never silent.

Inside the house my mother is packing
short sleeved shirts and faded bathing suits—
rubber clogs and flippers—
in a box marked SUMMER.

We are raking,
Dad and I.
Raking, raking.
The sky is blue, then orange, then gray.
My arms are tired.
I am dreaming of the box marked SUMMER.

# Carry Go

**by Vyanne Samuels**

**illustrated by Jennifer Northway**

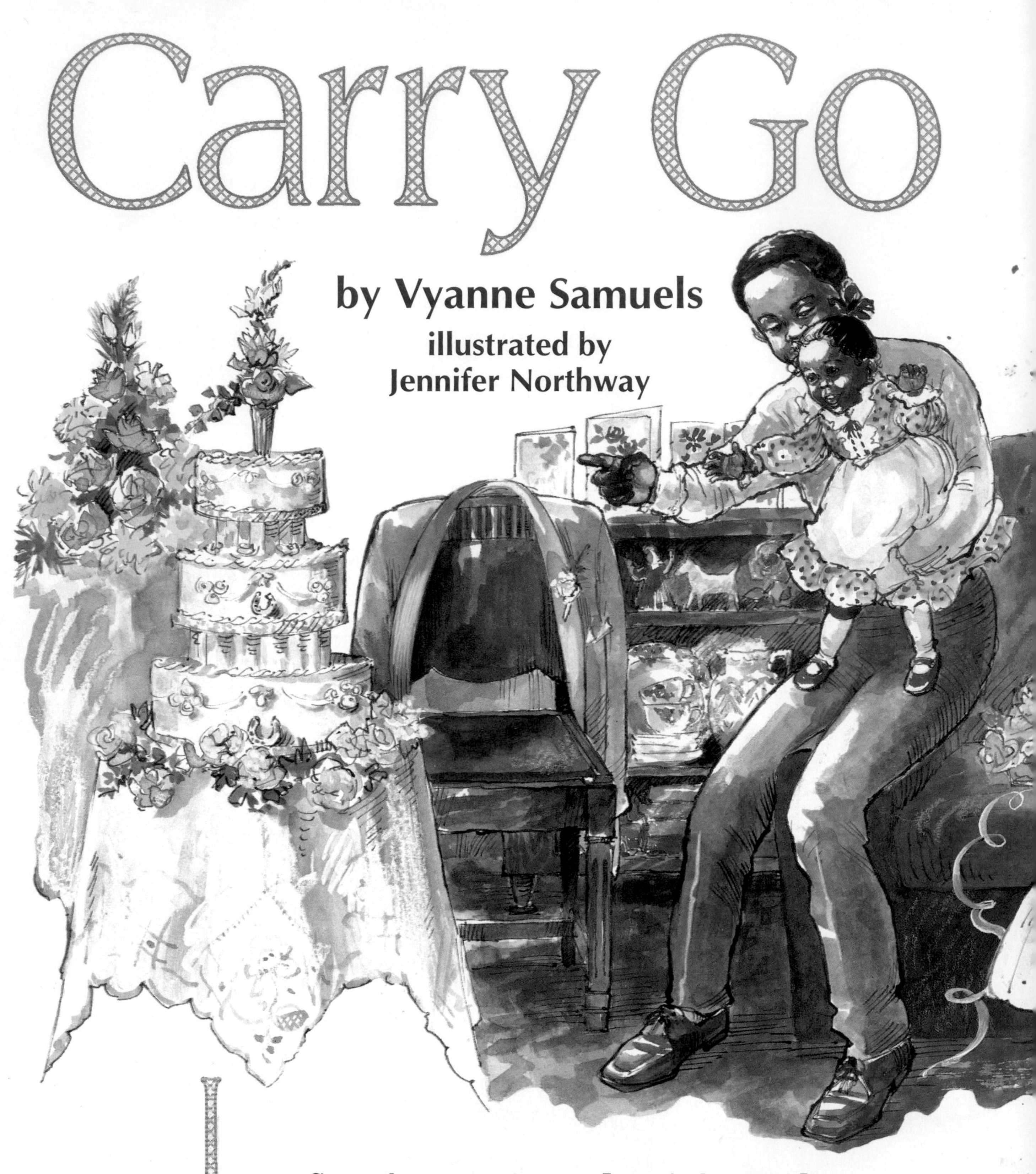

It was Saturday morning at Leon's house. It was a big Saturday morning at Leon's house. It was Marcia's wedding day. Marcia was Leon's sister.

# Bring Come

Everyone in the house was getting ready for the big Saturday morning. Everyone was getting ready for the big wedding.

Everyone, that is, except Leon, who was fast asleep downstairs.

"Wake up, Leon!" shouted his mother upstairs. But Leon did not move.

"Wake up, Leon!" shouted his sister Marlene upstairs.

But Leon did not move.

Leon's mother and his sisters, Marlene and Marcia, were so busy taking big blue rollers out of their hair that they forgot to shout at Leon to wake up again.

They were getting ready for the big day. They were getting ready for Marcia's wedding.

"Wake up, Leon," said Grandma softly downstairs.

Leon's two eyes opened up immediately.

Leon was awake.

"Carry this up to your mother," said Grandma, handing him a pink silk flower.

Leon ran upstairs to the bedroom with the pink silk flower. But before he could knock on the door, his sister Marcia called to him.

"Wait a little," she said, and she handed him a white veil. "Carry this down to Grandma."

So Leon put the flower between his teeth and the veil in his two hands and ran down the stairs to Grandma.

When he got to his grandma's door, she called to him before he could knock. "Wait a little," she said. He waited.

"Carry these up to Marlene," she said, and she poked a pair of blue shoes out at him.

So Leon put the veil on his head, kept the flower between his teeth, and carried the shoes in his two hands.

He tripped upstairs to Marlene.

But when he got to the bedroom door, Marlene called to him before he could knock.

"Wait a little," she said, and she poked a pair of yellow gloves through the door. "Carry these down to Grandma."

So Leon put the gloves on his hands,

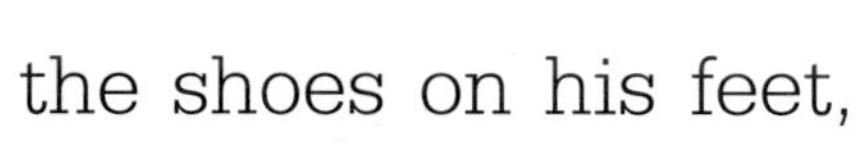

the shoes on his feet,

the veil on his head, and the pink silk flower between his teeth.

He wobbled downstairs to Grandma, who called to him before he could knock.

"Wait a little," she said. He waited.

"Carry this to Marcia," she said, and she poked a green bottle of perfume through the door.

"Mind how you go," she said.

So Leon climbed the stairs
carefully holding the green bottle of perfume,
carefully wearing the yellow gloves,
carefully dragging the blue shoes,
carefully balancing the white veil,
carefully biting the pink silk flower . . .
when suddenly he could go no further and shouted

**"HELP!"** from the middle of the stairs.

He nearly swallowed the flower.

His mother ran out of the room upstairs,
his sister Marlene ran out of the room upstairs,

and Grandma rushed out of her room downstairs.

There was a big silence. They all looked at Leon.

"Look 'pon his feet!" said his mother.
"Look 'pon his fingers and his hands!" said Marlene.
"Look 'pon his head!" said Grandma.
"Look 'pon his mouth!" said Marcia.
And they all let go a big laugh!

Leon looked like a bride!

One by one, Mother, Marcia, Marlene, and Grandma took away the pink silk flower, the white veil, the green bottle of perfume, the blue shoes, and the yellow gloves.

"When am I going to get dressed for the wedding?" asked Leon, wearing just his pajamas now.

"Just wait a little!" said Grandma.

Leon's two eyes opened wide.

"YOU MEAN I HAVE TO WAIT A LITTLE?" he shrieked.

And before anyone could answer, he ran downstairs . . .

and jumped straight back into his bed, without waiting even a little.

# Meet Vyanne Samuels

Vyanne Samuels got the idea for *Carry Go Bring Come* in a park in London, England, as she watched a child being asked to carry and fetch things.

Seeing this child reminded her of her home, Jamaica. She explains, "In Jamaica we say, 'You carry it to go' and 'You bring it to come.' *Carry Go Bring Come* means 'carrying and bringing things.'"

She says, "I wanted to write a story about what it is like in a West Indian household the morning of a wedding."

Ms. Samuels points out, "In the West Indies, the children are raised by the mother. Women take care of the child rearing, so there are no men in the story."

When Ms. Samuels wrote the book, her son, Dominic, was six years old. She says, "Dominic inspires ideas. After I finish writing a story, he tells me if it's funny or boring."

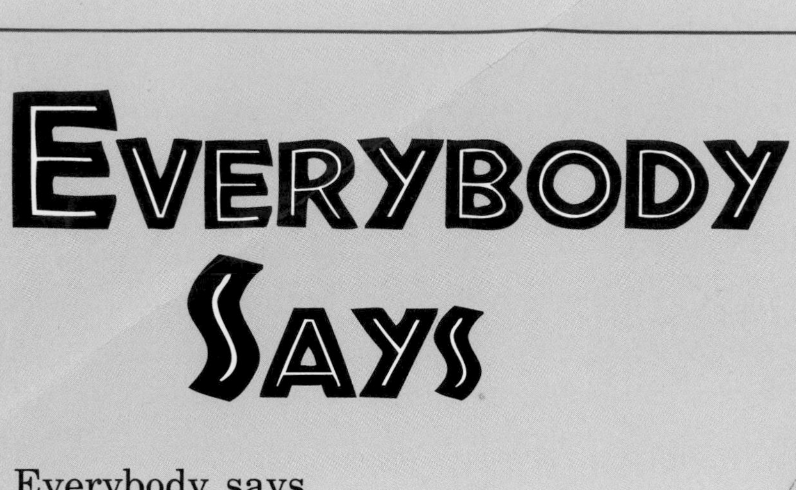

# Everybody Says

Everybody says
I look just like my mother.
Everybody says
I'm the image of Aunt Bee.
Everybody says
My nose is like my father's,
But *I* want to look like *me*.

*Dorothy Aldis*

HOME IS WHERE YOUR HEART IS
We Keep a Store
by ANNE SHELBY paintings by JOHN WARD

**We Keep a Store**
by Anne Shelby, illustrated by John Ward
Orchard Books, 1990

**Henry and Mudge and the Bedtime Thumps**
by Cynthia Rylant, illustrated by Suçie Stevenson
Bradbury Press, 1991

Amelia Bedelia's

# Family

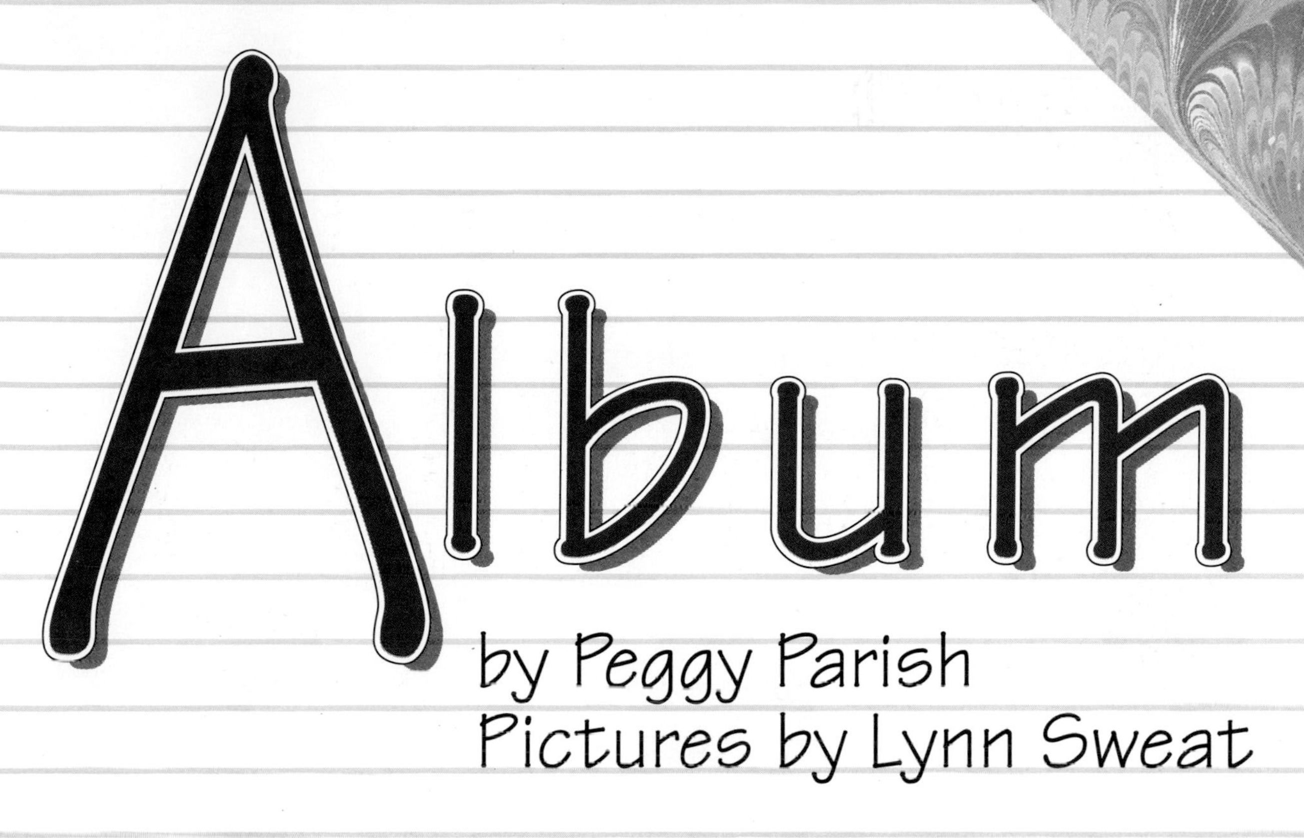

# Album

by Peggy Parish
Pictures by Lynn Sweat

"Amelia Bedelia," said Mrs. Rogers,
"you have been here a long time."

"Oh, Mrs. Rogers," said Amelia Bedelia,
"are you tired of me?"

"Of course not," said Mr. Rogers.
"We want to have a party for you.
We want to meet your family."

"Now that is nice," said Amelia Bedelia.

"Who would you like to invite?"
asked Mrs. Rogers.

"I'll get my family album,"
said Amelia Bedelia.
"You can help me decide."

"Good idea," said Mr. Rogers.
Amelia Bedelia got her album.

"This is my daddy,"
said Amelia Bedelia.
"He is a telephone operator."

"Then he helps people make calls,"
said Mr. Rogers.

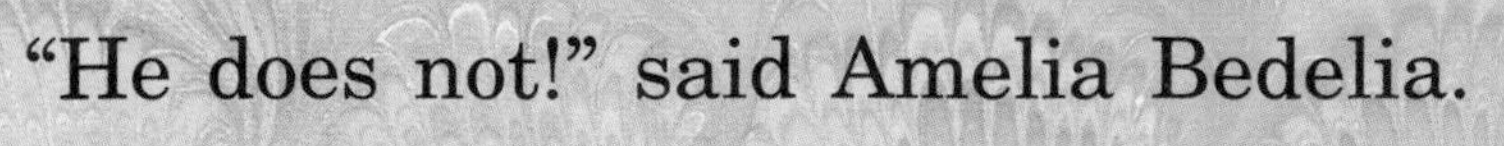

"He does not!" said Amelia Bedelia.
"He operates on telephones."

"I see," said Mr. Rogers.

"This is my mama,"
said Amelia Bedelia.
"She is a loafer."

"You mean she does nothing,"
said Mrs. Rogers.

"Certainly not," said Amelia Bedelia.
"She works hard. She makes
dough into loaves of bread.
That's what a loafer does."

"I see," said Mrs. Rogers.

"This is Uncle Albert,"
said Amelia Bedelia.
"He is a big-game hunter."

"You mean he kills animals?"
asked Mrs. Rogers.

"Why would he do that!"
said Amelia Bedelia.
"He hunts big games.
He has one so big
it takes up a whole room."

"I see," said Mrs. Rogers.

"Cousin Edward
is a horse racer,"
said Amelia Bedelia.

"Oh, he is a jockey,"
said Mr. Rogers.

"I don't think so," said Amelia Bedelia.
"Cousin Edward races horses.
He almost won once.
But he tripped and fell."

"I see," said Mr. Rogers.

"Uncle Dan takes pictures,"
said Amelia Bedelia.

"What kind of pictures
does he take?" asked Mr. Rogers.

"Any kind," said Amelia Bedelia.
"You really have to watch him.
He will take every picture
in the house."

"I see," said Mr. Rogers.

"My brother Ike
wants an orange grove,"
said Amelia Bedelia,
"but he has had bad luck."

"How is that?"
asked Mr. Rogers.

"He orders orange trees,"
said Amelia Bedelia,
"but they all come out green."

"I see," said Mr. Rogers.

"Cousin Clara is a bookkeeper," said Amelia Bedelia.

"She must be good with numbers," said Mr. Rogers.

"No," said Amelia Bedelia.
"But she is good at keeping books.
She never returns one."

"I see," said Mr. Rogers.

"Uncle Alf is a garbage collector,"
said Amelia Bedelia.

"That is smelly work,"
said Mr. Rogers.

"It sure is," said Amelia Bedelia.
"All of his neighbors moved away."

"I see," said Mr. Rogers.

"Cousin Susan belongs
to a fan club,"
said Amelia Bedelia.

"Are there many fans in her club?"
asked Mr. Rogers.

"Oh yes," said Amelia Bedelia.
"You never saw so many
different kinds of fans."

"I see," said Mr. Rogers.

"The last picture is of Ollie,"
said Amelia Bedelia.
"He is my nephew.
Ollie is our catcher."

"What does he catch?" asked Mr. Rogers.

"Everything," said Amelia Bedelia.
"Measles, mumps, colds.
Whatever comes along,
Ollie catches it."

"What an unusual family,"
said Mrs. Rogers.

"Yes," said Mr. Rogers.
"Invite all of them to the party."

"All right," said Amelia Bedelia.
She left the room.

In a bit she came back.
"They will be here tomorrow,"
she said.

"Tomorrow!" said Mrs. Rogers.
"We can't get everything ready by then."

"What's to get ready?"
asked Amelia Bedelia.

"Food!" said Mr. Rogers.

"Now, Mr. Rogers," said Amelia Bedelia,
"my folks know about parties.
They will bring the food."

"But Amelia Bedelia," said Mrs. Rogers,
"will there be enough food for everybody?"

"Everybody!" said Amelia Bedelia.
"I hadn't thought of inviting everybody.
What a good idea!"

She ran outside.
"Hear! Hear!" she shouted.
"A party tomorrow.
Everybody come."

And everybody came!

## Meet Peggy Parish

Peggy Parish loved teaching, but after many years, she stopped teaching and decided to write stories for children. She wrote more than thirty books for children. The best-known books are about a character named Amelia Bedelia.

Ms. Parish said about her writing, "Usually a book takes a lot of thinking, planning, and just hard work in writing and rewriting time and time again before it's ready to be published."

---

## Meet Lynn Sweat

When Lynn Sweat was asked about drawing the pictures for *Amelia Bedelia's Family Album,* he said, "The illustrations for this book were easy to do. The most difficult page in the book was the whole family on the hillside. I had to draw sixty to seventy people!"

**Did you ever see. . . .**

a house plant?

a butter fly?

a train ride?

a screw driver?

a home run?

*Knock! Knock!*

Who's there?

*Canoe.*

Canoe who?

*Canoe come out*

*and play with me?*

***Knock! Knock!***

**Who's there?**

***Boo.***

**Boo who?**

***Why are you crying?***

*Knock! Knock!*

Who's there?

*Banana.*

Banana who?

*Knock! Knock!*

Who's there?

*Banana.*

Banana who?

*Knock! Knock!*

Who's there?

*Orange.*

Orange who?

*Orange you glad*

*I didn't say banana?*

Knock! Knock! jokes are easy to write.
Use words that sound a little like other words,
and you have a Knock! Knock! joke!

# Meet Carmen Lomas Garza

Carmen Lomas Garza painted the pictures for *Family Pictures.* Then she told the story that described each picture.

Carmen Lomas Garza speaks both English and Spanish. She says, "First I learned Spanish. Then I learned English. But as I grew up, the Spanish language was always around me."

She says about the art in *Family Pictures:* "These paintings are about the first twenty years of my life. I painted them to feel proud of my Mexican-American background. I wanted to share it so other Mexican Americans can feel proud, too. I also think it's important for other people to look at the pictures and learn what it is like to be Mexican American."

Ms. Garza's mother was an artist, too. She says that when she was eight years old, she saw her mother painting pictures. "I thought she was doing magic," Ms. Garza said. "I decided I wanted to do the same thing. When everyone else was watching TV or napping, I was drawing."

# FAMILY

# PICTURES

## CUADROS de FAMILIA

by Carmen Lomas Garza

## The Fair in Reynosa

My friends and I once went to a very big fair across the border in Reynosa, Mexico. The fair lasted a whole week. Artisans and entertainers came from all over Mexico. There were lots of booths with food and crafts. This is one little section where everybody is ordering and eating tacos.

I painted a father buying tacos and the rest of the family sitting down at the table. The little girl is the father's favorite and that's why she gets to tag along with him. I can always recognize little girls who are their fathers' favorites.

## La Feria en Reynosa

Una vez, mis amigos y yo fuimos a una feria muy grande en Reynosa, México, al otro lado de la frontera. La feria duró una semana entera. Vinieron artesanos y artistas de todo México. Había muchos puestos que vendían comida y artesanías. Ésta es una pequeña parte de la feria donde todos están comprando tacos y comiéndoselos.

Pinté a un padre comprando tacos y al resto de la familia sentada a la mesa. La niñita pequeña es la preferida de su papá, y por eso es que él la permite acompañarlo. Aún hoy, siempre puedo reconocer cuando una niñita es la preferida de su papá.

SODAS
CocaCola
Fresa $5.00 pesos
Limon
CARNE
ASADA
Con Tomate
y
Salsa $12.00 pesos
CARMEN LOMAS
©1987
La feria en Re

## Oranges

We were always going to my grandparents' house, so whatever they were involved in we would get involved in. In this picture my grandmother is hanging up the laundry. We told her that the oranges needed picking so she said, "Well, go ahead and pick some." Before she knew it, she had too many oranges to hold in her hands, so she made a basket out of her apron. That's my brother up in the tree, picking oranges. The rest of us are picking up the ones that he dropped on the ground.

## Naranjas

Siempre íbamos a la casa de mis abuelos, así que cualquier cosa que estuvieran haciendo ellos, nosotros la hacíamos también. En este cuadro, mi abuela está colgando la ropa a secar. Nosotros le dijimos que las naranjas estaban listas para cosechar, y ella nos respondió: —Vayan pues, recójanlas. En un dos por tres, tenía demasiadas naranjas para sostenerlas en las manos, así que convirtió su delantal en canasta. Ése es mi hermano, en el árbol, recogiendo naranjas. El resto de nosotros estamos recogiendo las que él deja caer al suelo.

## For Dinner

This is my grandparents' backyard. My grandmother is killing a chicken for dinner. My grandfather is in the chicken coop trying to catch another chicken. Later, my family will sit down to eat Sunday dinner—chicken soup.

That's me in the blue dress with my younger brother, Arturo. He was so surprised by the scene that he started to spill his snowcone. We had never seen anything like that before. I knew my grandparents had always raised chickens, but I never knew how the chickens got to be soup.

## Para la cena

Éste es el patio de mis abuelos. Mi abuela está matando a una gallina para la cena. Mi abuelo está en el gallinero tratando de atrapar a otra gallina. Más tarde, mi familia se sentará a comer la cena del domingo: sopa de pollo.

Ésa soy yo, vestida de azul, con mi hermano menor, Arturo. Él estaba tan sorprendido por lo que veía que se le empezó a derramar su raspa. Nunca antes habíamos visto algo parecido. Yo sabía que mis abuelos criaban gallinas, pero no había sabido antes cómo era que las gallinas se convertían en sopa.

CARMEN LOMAS
©1996

## Birthday Party

That's me hitting the piñata at my sixth birthday party. It was also my brother's fourth birthday. My mother made a big birthday party for us and invited all kinds of friends, cousins and neighborhood kids.

You can't see the piñata when you're trying to hit it, because your eyes are covered with a handkerchief. My father is pulling the rope that makes the piñata go up and down. He will make sure that everybody has a chance to hit it at least once. Somebody will end up breaking it, and that's when all the candies will fall out and all the kids will run and try to grab them.

## Cumpleaños

Ésa soy yo, pegándole a la piñata en la fiesta que me dieron cuando cumplí seis años. Era también el cumpleaños de mi hermano, que cumplía cuatro años. Mi madre nos dio una gran fiesta e invitó a muchos primos, vecinos y amigos.

No puedes ver la piñata cuando le estás dando con el palo, porque tienes los ojos cubiertos por un pañuelo. Mi padre está tirando de la cuerda que sube y baja la piñata. Él se encargará de que todos tengan por lo menos una oportunidad de pegarle a la piñata. Luego alguien acabará rompiéndola, y entonces todos los caramelos que tiene dentro caerán y todos los niños correrán a cogerlos.

Happy Birthday Carmen
Happy Birthday

1 5 7 4 3 15 12 8 11 2 5 13 4

## Cakewalk

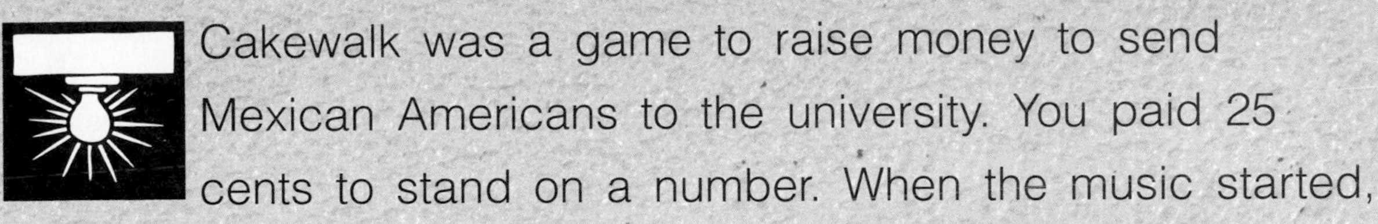

Cakewalk was a game to raise money to send Mexican Americans to the university. You paid 25 cents to stand on a number. When the music started, you walked around and around. When the music stopped, whatever number you happened to step on was your number. Then one of the ladies in the center would pick out a number from the can. If you were standing on the winning number, you would win a cake. That's my mother in the center of the circle in the pink and black dress. My father is serving punch. I'm the little girl in front of the store scribbling on the sidewalk with a twig.

## Cakewalk

Cakewalk era un juego que se hacía para recaudar fondos para darles becas universitarias a jóvenes méxico-americanos. Se pagaba 25 centavos para poder pararse sobre un número. Cuando la música empezaba a tocar, todos empezaban a caminar en círculo. Cuando se terminaba la música, el número sobre el cual estabas parado era tu número. Entonces una de las señoras que estaba en el centro del círculo escogía un número de la lata. Si estabas parado sobre el número de la suerte, ganabas un pastel. Ésa es mi madre en el centro del círculo, vestida de rosado y negro. Mi papá esta sirviendo ponche. Yo soy la niñita dibujando garabatos en la acera al frente de la tienda con una ramita.

## Picking Nopal Cactus

In the early spring my grandfather would come and get us and we'd all go out into the woods to pick nopal cactus. My grandfather and my mother are slicing off the fresh, tender leaves of the nopal and putting them in boxes. My grandmother and my brother Arturo are pulling leaves from the mesquite tree to line the boxes. After we got home my grandfather would shave off all the needles from each leaf of cactus. Then my grandmother would parboil the leaves in hot water. The next morning she would cut them up and stir fry them with chili powder and eggs for breakfast.

## Piscando nopalitos

Al comienzo de la primavera, mi abuelo nos venía a buscar y todos íbamos al bosque a piscar nopalitos. Mi abuelo y mi madre están cortando las pencas tiernas del nopal y metiéndolas en cajas. Mi abuela y mi hermano Arturo están recogiendo hojas de mesquite para forrar las cajas. Después que regresábamos a casa, mi abuelo le quitaba las espinas a cada penca del cactus. Luego mi abuela cocía las pencas en agua hirviente. A la mañana siguiente, las cortaba y las freía con chile y huevos para nuestro desayuno.

Rio Grande
OJAS
CARMEN LOMAS GARZA
©1987
TAMALADA

## Making Tamales

This is a scene from my parents' kitchen. Everybody is making tamales. My grandfather is wearing blue overalls and a blue shirt. I'm right next to him with my sister Margie. We're helping to soak the dried leaves from the corn. My mother is spreading the cornmeal dough on the leaves and my aunt and uncle are spreading meat on the dough. My grandmother is lining up the rolled and folded tamales ready for cooking. In some families just the women make tamales, but in our family everybody helps.

## La Tamalada

Ésta es una escena de la cocina de mis padres. Todos están haciendo tamales. Mi abuelo tiene puesto rancheros azules y camisa azul. Yo estoy al lado de él, con mi hermana Margie. Estamos ayudando a remojar las hojas secas del maíz. Mi mamá está esparciendo la masa de maíz sobre las hojas, y mis tíos están esparciendo la carne sobre la masa. Mi abuelita está ordenando los tamales que ya están enrollados, cubiertos y listos para cocer. En algunas familias sólo las mujeres preparan tamales, pero en mi familia todos ayudan.

## Watermelon

It's a hot summer evening. The whole family's on the front porch. My grandfather had brought us some watermelons that afternoon. We put them in the refrigerator and let them chill down. After supper we went out to the front porch. My father cut the watermelon and gave each one of us a slice.

It was fun to sit out there. The light was so bright on the porch that you couldn't see beyond the edge of the lit area. It was like being in our own little world.

## Sandía

Es una noche calurosa de verano. Toda la familia está en el corredor. Mi abuelo nos había traído unas sandías esa tarde. Las pusimos en el refrigerador para enfriarlas. Despues de la cena, salimos al corredor. Mi padre cortó la sandía y nos dio un pedazo a cada uno.

Era divertido estar sentados allá afuera. La luz del corredor era tan fuerte que no se podía ver más allá del área que estaba iluminada. Era como estar en nuestro propio pequeño mundo.

CARMEN
LOMAS
GARZA
© 1985

## Beds for Dreaming

My sister and I used to go up on the roof on summer nights and just stay there and talk about the stars and the constellations. We also talked about the future. I knew since I was 13 years old that I wanted to be an artist. And all those things that I dreamed of doing as an artist, I'm finally doing now. My mother was the one who inspired me to be an artist. She made up our beds to sleep in and have regular dreams, but she also laid out the bed for our dreams of the future.

## Camas para soñar

Mi hermana y yo solíamos subirnos al techo en las noches de verano y nos quedábamos allí platicando sobre las estrellas y las constelaciones. También platicábamos del futuro. Yo sabía desde que tenía trece años que quería ser artista. Y todas las cosas que soñaba hacer como artista, por fin las estoy haciendo ahora. Mi madre fue la que me inspiró a ser artista. Ella nos tendía las camas para que durmiéramos y tuviéramos sueños normales, pero también preparó la cuna para nuestros sueños del futuro.

Dad
mom
Cousins
Aunt and Uncle
Brother
Brownie

# RELATIVES

BY JEFF MOSS

(A Poem To Say Fast When You Want To Show Off)

My father's and mother's sisters and brothers
Are called my uncles and aunts
(Except when they're called *ma tante* and *mon oncle*
Which happens if they're in France.)
Now the daughters and sons of my uncles and aunts
Are my cousins. (Confusion increases—
Since if you're my mother or if you're my Dad,
Then those cousins are nephews and nieces.)

**pictures by Fannellie Ann Ortiz**
**second grader**

# CONTENTS

UNIT
2
NOW I KNOW!

A
Kettle's for the kitchen,
A key is for the door,
A kitten is for playing with
And keeping on the floor.

A kite is made for flying
When March winds blow,
Kindness is for everyone—
Didn't you know?

MARGARET AND JOHN TRAVERS MOORE

# Meet Joyce Durham Barrett

"The idea for *Willie's Not the Hugging Kind* came from two boys I knew—Willie and Anthony," explains Joyce Durham Barrett. "On the way home from the library, I stopped by to visit my sister, and I was hugging everyone there. When I got to my nephew, Anthony, he jumped up saying, 'No, no! I'm not the hugging kind!' Anthony's words got mixed up with the boy Willie, and that's how I came up with the story."

# Meet Pat Cummings

Pat Cummings used people she knew as models for the illustrations in *Willie's Not the Hugging Kind.* "Knowing and caring about the models helps me to show the warmth and caring of the family in the story."

When asked how she drew the pictures for this book, Pat Cummings said, "The first thing I did was think about what pictures I wanted to illustrate. Then I made sketches of what I wanted to show. Then I had the models pose for me like the sketches, and I took photographs of the models. Later on I drew the illustrations."

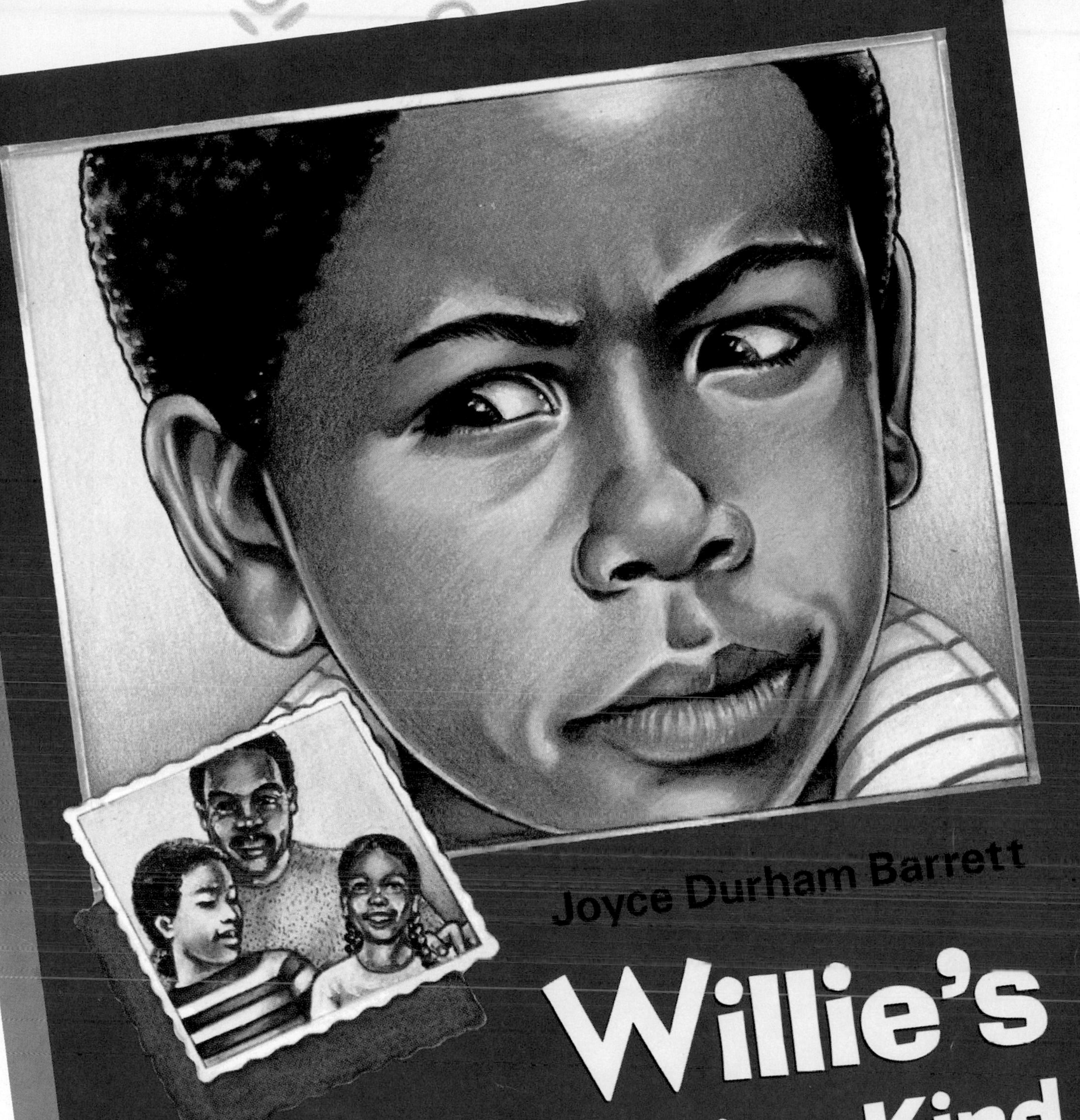

Joyce Durham Barrett

# Willie's Not the Hugging Kind

illustrated by Pat Cummings

Willie wanted someone to hug. That's what he wanted more than anything.

But no one hugged Willie. Not anymore.

Not even his daddy when he dropped Willie and his friend Jo-Jo off at school. Now, he just patted Willie on the head and said, "See you around, Son."

Willie didn't like to be patted on the head. It made him feel like a little dog. Besides, hugging felt much nicer, no matter what Jo-Jo said.

Every day Jo-Jo rode to school in the linen truck with Willie and his daddy. And when Willie used to hug his daddy good-bye, Jo-Jo would turn his head and laugh. "What did you do that for? Man, that's silly," Jo-Jo would say once they had crawled out of the truck.

TIFFANY PL
KANE ST
ONE WAY

So Willie stopped hugging his daddy. He never hugged his mama or his sister anymore either. And when they tried to hug Willie, he turned away. But Willie wanted someone to hug. That's what he wanted more than anything.

At school he watched as Miss Mary put her arms around some boy or girl. It didn't look silly. Except when she tried to hug Jo-Jo. Jo-Jo made a big commotion that made everyone laugh. He wriggled and squirmed, and shrieked, "Help! Help! I'm being mugged! Help!"

At night Willie watched his sister pull her teddy bear to her and hug it. She looked so safe and happy lying there with her arms around the bear.

"Why do you hug that old thing?" Willie said. "That's silly."

Rose frowned at Willie. "Who says?" she demanded.

"Jo-Jo says, that's who says," Willie boasted.

"Well, if you ask me, I think Jo-Jo's silly," said Rose. "Besides," she said, squeezing the bear to her, "Homer's nice."

But the next night Willie pinched his nose and said, "What a smelly old bear! I wouldn't hug that old thing for a hundred dollars. Not even for a million dollars. That's silly."

Rose pulled Homer in closer to her. "Willie," she said, "you're just not the hugging kind, then . . . if that's how you feel."

Willie flipped over in bed without even saying, "Good night, sleep tight, God keep you alright." And his mind went around and around on what his sister had said. The words tick-tocked back and forth with the clock sitting on the table by his bed:

NOT-the hugging kind,

NOT-the hugging kind,

NOT-the hugging kind,

if-THAT'S-how-you-feel.

But that was not how Willie felt. More than anything, Willie wanted to be the hugging kind.

Willie watched each morning as his daddy hugged first his mama and then Rose. He remembered how safe and happy he always felt with his daddy's strong arms around him.

He remembered how good it felt to put his arms around his mama. She smelled a little like lemon and a little like the lilac powder in the bathroom. She felt big and a little lumpy. She also felt soft and safe and warm.

One morning Willie went into the kitchen and everyone was hugging everyone else. But no one hugged Willie. They didn't even see him. Willie waited, hoping someone would put their arms around him. If they did, maybe he wouldn't slip away.

But no one tried. Rose just said, when she saw Willie watching, "You know that Willie says he isn't the hugging kind now. He says it's all too, too silly."

"I did not!" said Willie, bristling. "Jo-Jo said that!"

"Oh, but you said it too, Little Brother," Rose said, laughing and tousling his hair.

Willie grabbed his lunch and his books, and ran out the door to meet Jo-Jo. "Let's get out of here!" Willie shrieked, breaking into a run. "They're mugging everybody in there!"

That afternoon Jo-Jo's mother picked him up after school, so Willie walked home alone.

He walked through the park and saw a young couple standing on the footbridge with their arms around each other.

He walked down Myrtle Street and saw a woman and a man rushing down the steps from their porch to greet some visitors with hugs all around.

It seemed so long since Willie had had a hug.

He walked into the long, low branches of a willow tree and wrapped his arms around it. A blue jay flew down from a purple plum tree, and Willie reached out to its fluttering wings. He walked up to a stop sign and hugged it.

He hugged his bike in the front yard. He hugged the door to his house when he opened it. And he rushed inside to hug his mama. But she was too busy running the vacuum over the floors. Willie was kind of glad. After all, he felt a little silly.

That night, after Willie had had his bath, he took the old bath towel and draped it across the head of his bed.

"What's that for?" Rose asked, hugging Homer to her.

"Nothing," said Willie.

The next night Willie put the old bath towel on the bed again. And the next night, and the next. Each night, when he was sure that Rose was not watching, he slipped the old towel down from the headboard and he hugged it. But it didn't feel soft and safe and warm.

Willie wanted to hug someONE, not someTHING.

In the morning Willie's mama was in the kitchen making biscuits. He watched Rose brush up to her and put her arms around her.

When the biscuits were finished and browning in the oven, Willie went up and put his arms around his mama too. Or almost around her. There was a little more to her than he remembered. She felt much nicer than an old towel. And, even better, she hugged back.

"What's all this, Willie," she said, "hugging around here on me so early in the morning?"

"Yeah, Willie," said Rose. "I thought all that hugging was too, too silly."

Willie clung tighter to his mama.

"That's alright," said his mama. "Willie knows, don't you, Son, that it's them that don't get hugging who think it's silly."

Willie looked up into his mama's face, smiling, until he felt a tap on his shoulder. Turning, he saw his daddy smiling down at him. "My turn, Son," he said.

Willie put his arms around his daddy, burying his face in the familiar khaki shirt and feeling once again secure in the warmth of the strong arms around him.

Breakfast tasted better to Willie than it had in many a day. And when it came time to leave for school, Willie gave hugs all around.

Jumping into the big truck, Willie and his daddy stopped by to pick up Jo-Jo. When they arrived at school, Willie reached up and gave his daddy a quick, tight hug. Then he scooted out the door behind Jo-Jo.

"What did you do that for, man?" Jo-Jo said, once they were out of the truck. "Don't you know that's silly?"

Willie gave his friend a shove on the shoulder. Maybe Jo-Jo wouldn't let someone hug him, but he would allow a playful shove now and then. "Go on, now, Jo-Jo," he said. "I think *you're* what's silly."

Jo-Jo ran on ahead. "Help, help!" he shrieked. "I'm being mugged! Help!"

But Willie didn't mind. He lagged behind, feeling warm and safe knowing that he was, after all, the hugging kind.

*Hugs and hugs and kisses . . .*
Doesn't she know that I'm a boy?
*Hugs and hugs and kisses . . .*
I'm not some cuddly toy.

*Hugs and hugs and kisses . . .*
Boys should be treated rough.
*Hugs and hugs and kisses . . .*
These muscles show I'm tough.

*Hugs and hugs and kisses . . .*
Makes me want to run and hide.
I can't show the world how warm . . .
*hugs and hugs and kisses*
makes me feel
inside.

*Lindamichellebaron*

NEVER
KISS
AN
ALLIG

# ATOR!

COLLEEN STANLEY BARE

Never kiss an alligator,
hug an alligator,
pat, poke, push, hit, kick,
or even touch an alligator,
because alligators bite!

When you meet an alligator,
usually at a zoo,
what should you do?

Watch, look, and learn,
for alligators are fascinating!

Alligators are ancient,
and lived when the dinosaurs lived
about two hundred million years ago.

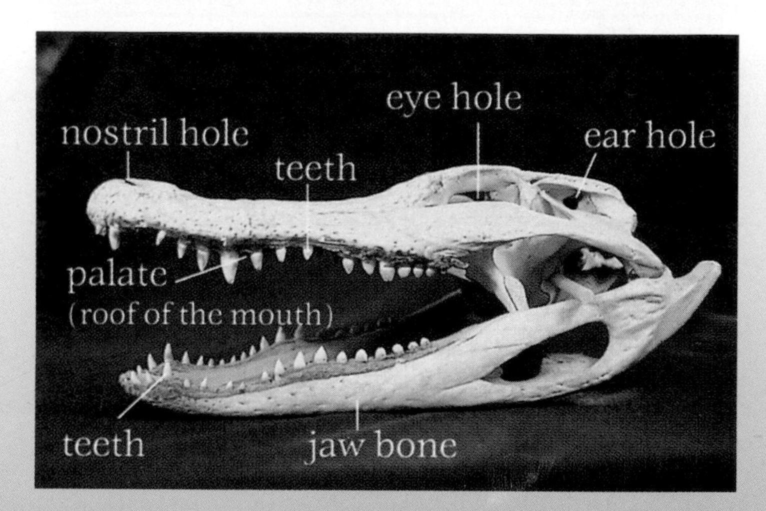


The name alligator is from a
Spanish word "el lagarto,"
which means "the lizard."
Lizards do look like miniature
alligators.

Alligators are found in only two
parts of the world:
a few in eastern China,
most in the warm
southeastern United States,
especially Louisiana and Florida.

Alligators live in water,
beside water
half in and half
out of water.

They stay in ponds,
beside an algae-covered pond
in an algae-covered pond

in swamps, marshes, lakes,
rivers, streams,
and sometimes in people's
swimming pools, fish ponds,
and in water on golf courses.

Alligators can stay under the
water at least an hour, holding
their breaths.
In dry seasons
they may dig deep holes in
the ground until they find
water.
These "gator holes" are also used
by other wildlife.

Alligators aren't crocodiles, and
crocodiles aren't alligators, although
they belong to the same family,
called Crocodilia (Crock-o-DILLy-uh).

Alligators have
broad, rounded
noses.

Alligators'
lower teeth don't
show when their
mouths are closed.

Crocodiles have
longer, skinnier
noses.

Crocodiles'
lower teeth do
show when their
mouths are closed.

Crocodiles are crankier, bolder,
fiercer,
and move faster than alligators,
so certainly, definitely, without a
doubt,
you should never kiss a
crocodile's snout!

Alligators have huge mouths,
with about eighty sharp teeth
for snapping and snatching:
insects, fish, small animals,
birds, turtles, frogs, snakes,
sometimes stones, bottle caps,
cans,

and even people, if people
tease or get in the way.

Alligator teeth fall out and get
replaced by new ones,
up to three thousand in a
fifty-year lifetime.

Alligators have short, stubby legs
for walking on land
and, for a brief distance, can run
as fast as you can.

Alligators have long, scaly tails for swimming in water.

The faster they swish their tails,
the faster they can swim.

Alligators' eyes, ears, and noses
are on top of their heads,
so they can see, hear, and smell
while they hide in the water
to watch for meals.

Where is the alligator?

There is the alligator.

Alligators are reptiles,
so their body temperatures are
the same as the air or the
water around them.
They lie around looking lazy
to get warm in the sun,
to get cool in the shade.

Like most reptiles, mother
alligators lay eggs.
Babies hatch out of the thirty to
sixty eggs
in about ten weeks.

Newborn alligators are eight to
nine inches long
and have sharp little teeth that
nip and bite.

So never kiss a baby alligator,
either!

Colleen Bare has always been fascinated with alligators. She says, "Some people think alligators are ugly, but the scaly skin that makes them ugly has made it possible for them to survive since the age of dinosaurs. Alligators are really beautiful to those who love them."

Ms. Bare travels all around the world taking photographs of wild animals. "I love photographing wildlife and writing about it," she says. "It is my favorite thing to do!"

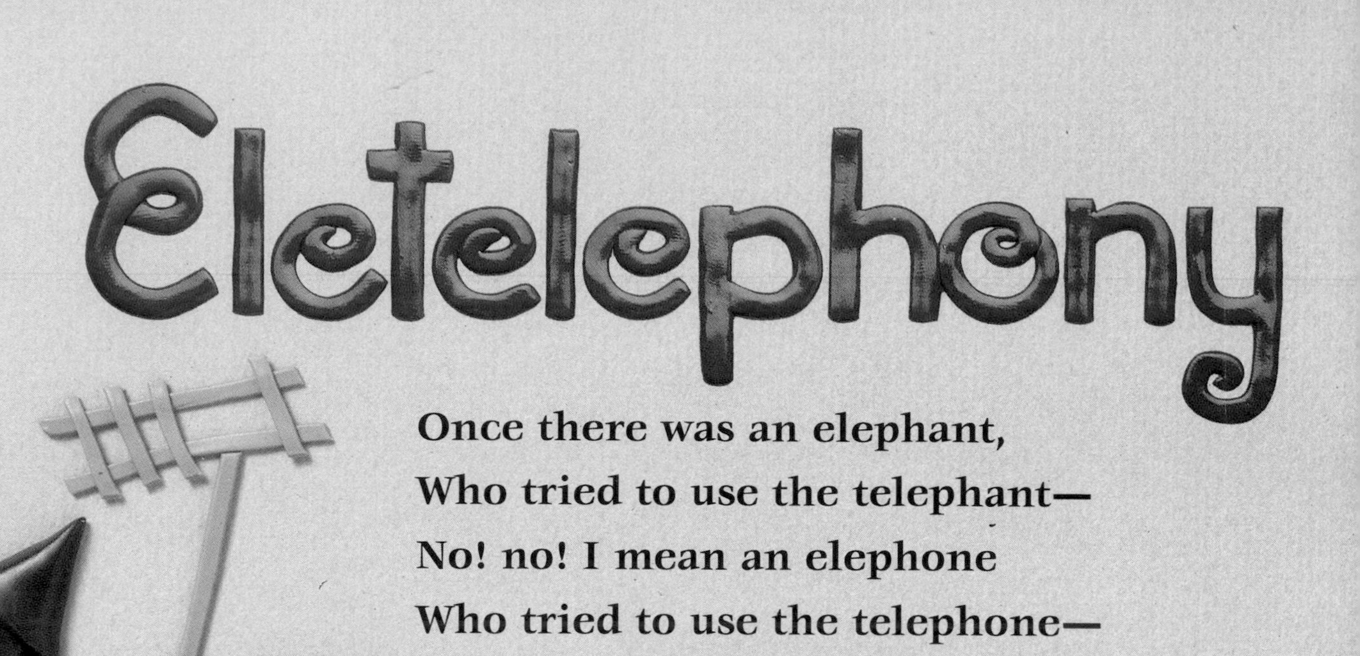

# Eletelephony

Once there was an elephant,
Who tried to use the telephant—
No! no! I mean an elephone
Who tried to use the telephone—
(Dear me! I am not certain quite
That even now I've got it right.)

Howe'er it was, he got his trunk
Entangled in the telephunk;
The more he tried to get it free,
The louder buzzed the telephee—
(I fear I'd better drop the song
Of elephop and telephong!)

*Laura E. Richards*

TELEPHONE

# What Do You Know?

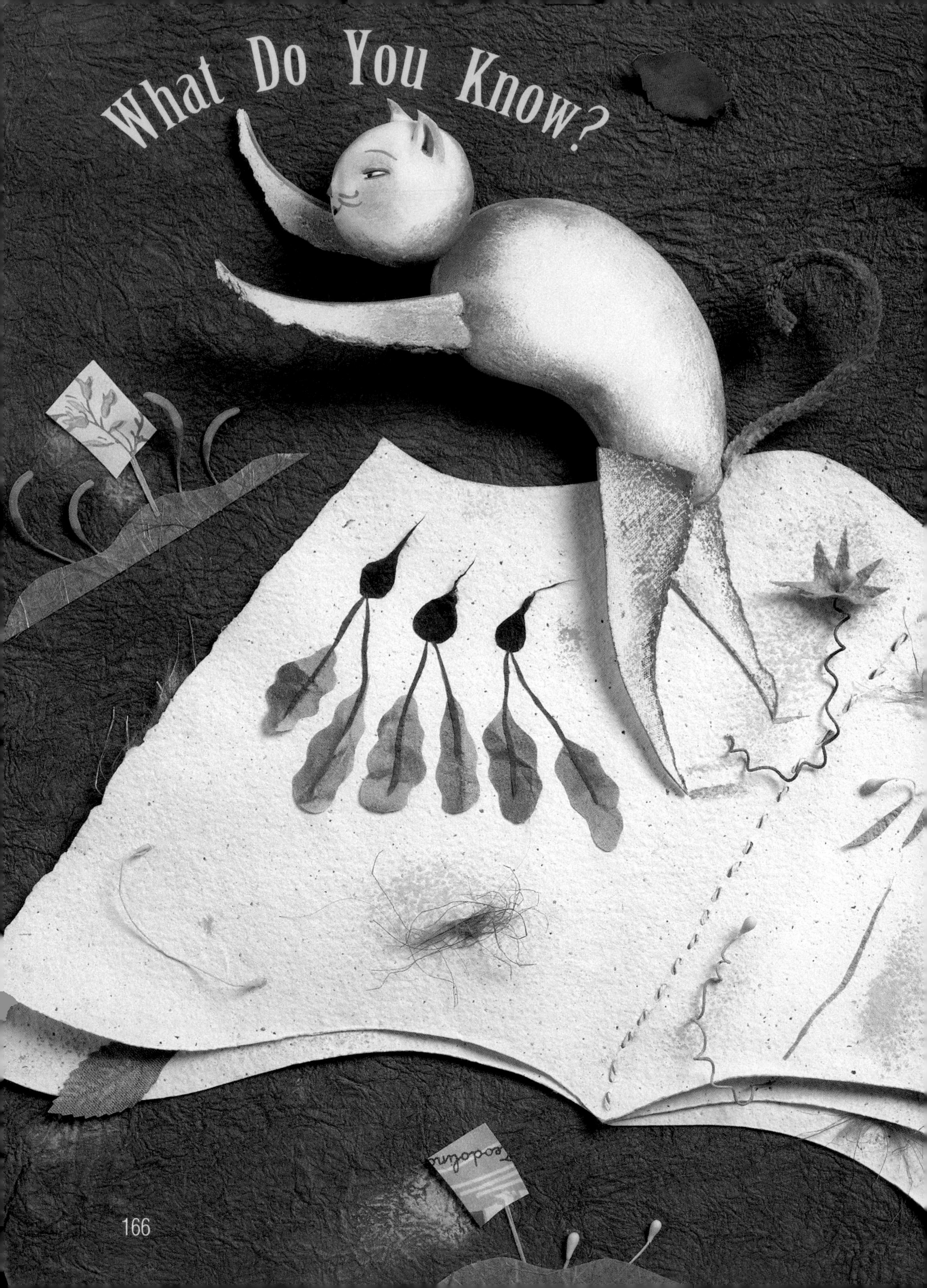

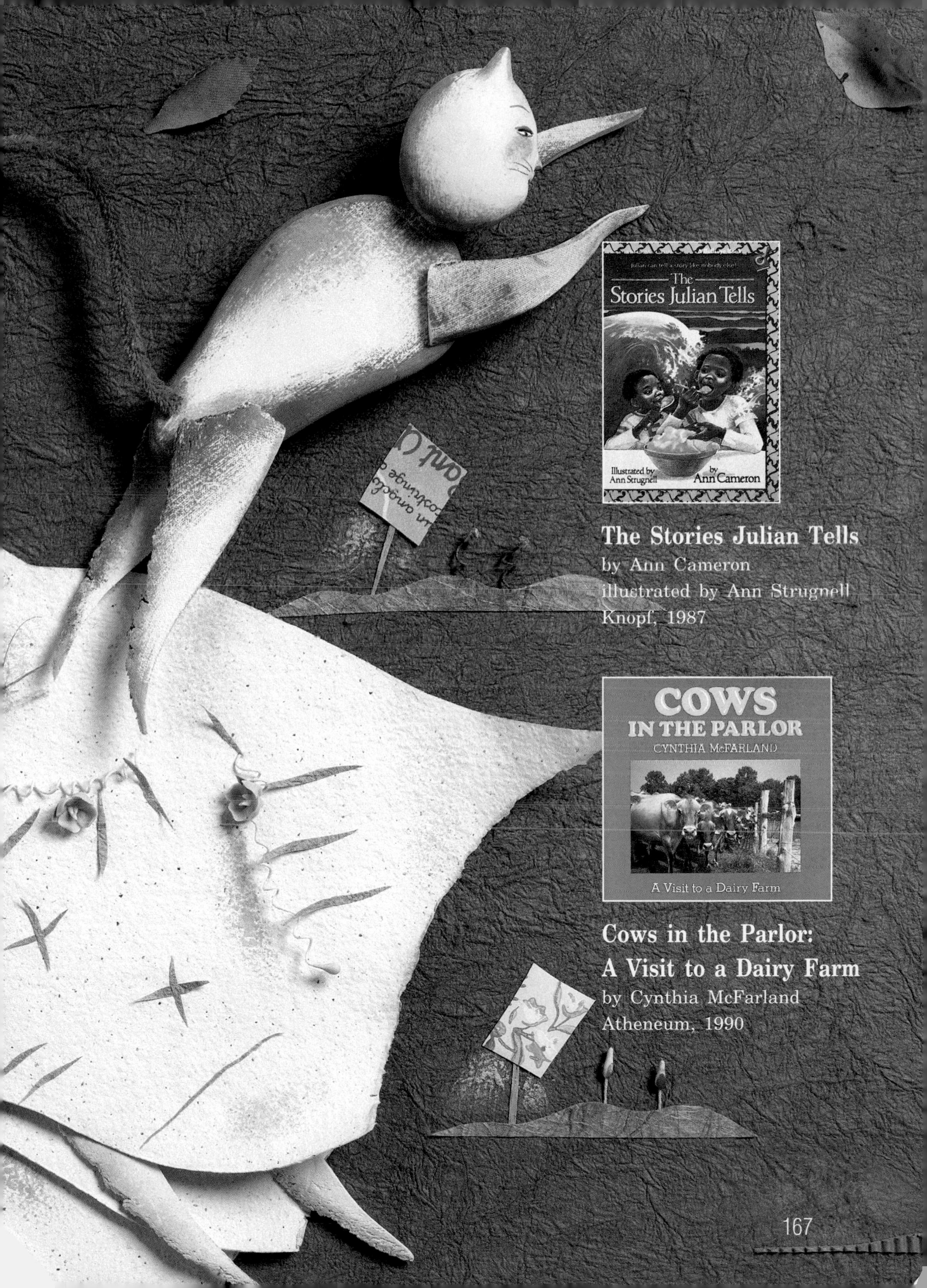


**The Stories Julian Tells**
by Ann Cameron
illustrated by Ann Strugnell
Knopf, 1987

**Cows in the Parlor: A Visit to a Dairy Farm**
by Cynthia McFarland
Atheneum, 1990

A FOLK TALE FROM THE HMONG PEOPLE OF LAOS
TOLD BY BLIA XIONG

# NINE-IN-ONE, GRR! GRR!

ADAPTED BY CATHY SPAGNOLI
ILLUSTRATED BY NANCY HOM

Many years ago when the earth was nearer the sky than it is today, there lived the first tiger. She and her mate had no babies and so the lonely tiger often thought about the future, wondering how many cubs she would have.

Tiger decided to visit the great god Shao, who lived in the sky, who was kind and gentle and knew everything. Surely Shao could tell her how many cubs she would have.

Tiger set out on the road that led to the sky. She climbed through forests of striped bamboo and wild banana trees, past plants curved like rooster tail feathers, and over rocks shaped like sleeping dragons.

At last Tiger came to a stone wall. Beyond the wall was a garden where children played happily under a plum tree. A large house stood nearby, its colorful decorations shining in the sun. This was the land of the great Shao, a peaceful land without sickness or death.

Shao himself came out to greet Tiger. The silver coins dangling from his belt sounded softly as he walked.

"Why did you come here, Tiger?" he asked gently.

"O great Shao," answered Tiger respectfully, "I am lonely and want to know how many cubs I will have."

Shao was silent for a moment. Then he replied, "Nine each year."

"How wonderful," purred Tiger. "Thank you so much, great Shao." And she turned to leave with her good news.

"One moment, Tiger," said Shao. "You must remember carefully what I said. The words alone tell you how many cubs you will have. Do not forget them, for if you do, I cannot help you."

At first Tiger was happy as she followed the road back to earth. But soon, she began to worry.

"Oh dear," she said to herself. "My memory is so bad. How will I ever remember those important words of Shao?" She thought and she thought. At last, she had an idea. "I'll make up a little song to sing. Then I won't forget." So Tiger began to sing:

**Nine-in-one, Grr! Grr!**
**Nine-in-one, Grr! Grr!**

Down the mountain went Tiger, past the rocks shaped like sleeping dragons, past the plants curved like rooster tail feathers, through the forests of striped bamboo and wild banana trees. Over and over she sang her song:

**Nine-in-one, Grr! Grr!**
**Nine-in-one, Grr! Grr!**

As Tiger came closer to her cave, she passed through clouds of tiny white butterflies. She heard monkeys and barking deer. She saw green-striped snakes, quails and pheasants. None of the animals listened to her song—except one big, clever, black bird, the Eu bird.

"Hmm," said Bird to herself. "I wonder why Tiger is coming down the mountain singing that song and grinning from ear to ear. I'd better find out." So Bird soared up the ladder which was a shortcut to Shao's home.

"O wise Shao," asked Bird politely, "why is Tiger singing over and over:

**Nine-in-one, Grr! Grr!**
**Nine-in-one, Grr! Grr!**

And Shao explained that he had just told Tiger she would have nine cubs each year.

"That's terrible!" squawked Bird. "If Tiger has nine cubs each year, they will eat all of us. Soon there will be nothing but tigers in the land. You must change what you said, O Shao!"

"I cannot take back my words," sighed Shao. "I promised Tiger that she would have nine cubs every year as long as she remembered my words."

"As long as she remembered your words," repeated Bird thoughtfully. "Then I know what I must do, O great Shao."

Bird now had a plan. She could hardly wait to try it out. Quickly, she returned to earth in search of Tiger.

Bird reached her favorite tree as old grandmother sun was setting, just in time to hear Tiger coming closer and closer and still singing:

**Nine-in-one, Grr! Grr!**
**Nine-in-one, Grr! Grr!**

Tiger was concentrating so hard on her song that she didn't even see Bird landing in the tree above her.

Suddenly, Bird began to flap her wings furiously. "Flap! Flap! Flap!" went Bird's big, black wings.

"Who's that?" cried Tiger.

"It's only me," answered Bird innocently.

Tiger looked up and growled at Bird:

"Grr! Grr! Bird. You made me forget my song with all your noise."

"Oh, I can help you," chirped Bird sweetly. "I heard you walking through the woods. You were singing:

**One-in-nine, Grr! Grr!**
**One-in-nine, Grr! Grr!**

"Oh, thank you, thank you, Bird!" cried Tiger. "I will have one cub every nine years. How wonderful! This time I won't forget!"

So Tiger returned to her cave, singing happily:

**One-in-nine, Grr! Grr!**
**One-in-nine, Grr! Grr!**

And that is why, the Hmong people say, we don't have too many tigers on the earth today!

# MEET BLIA XIONG

Blia Xiong (BLEE-AH SHONG) first heard ***Nine-in-One, Grr! Grr!*** when she was a little child. She says, "This story was carried in my family for a long time. I was three when I first heard it. I still remember my mother telling me this funny story with a tiger singing in Laotian, 'Nine-in-One, Grr! Grr!'"

In Laos, the tiger is a wild animal that is feared. Some people think the tiger is magical. She says, "The part I like most is when the bird hears the song and figures out how to trick the tiger. The clever bird does something about the powerful tiger."

Blia Xiong was told stories by her mother, her father, and her grandfather before them. Now she tells her children the stories she hears. When asked how she remembers a story, she says, "When I listen to a story, I listen very closely. I make pictures in my mind. Then I can remember what I hear."

# MEET NANCY HOM

Nancy Hom was born in southern China and grew up in New York City. In addition to *Nine-in-One, Grr! Grr!* she has illustrated the Cambodian folk tale *Judge Rabbit and the Tree Spirit.*

A Look at
LAOS
ARCTIC OCEAN
CANADIAN SHIELD
NORTH AMERICA
NORTH ATLANTIC OCEAN
OCEAN

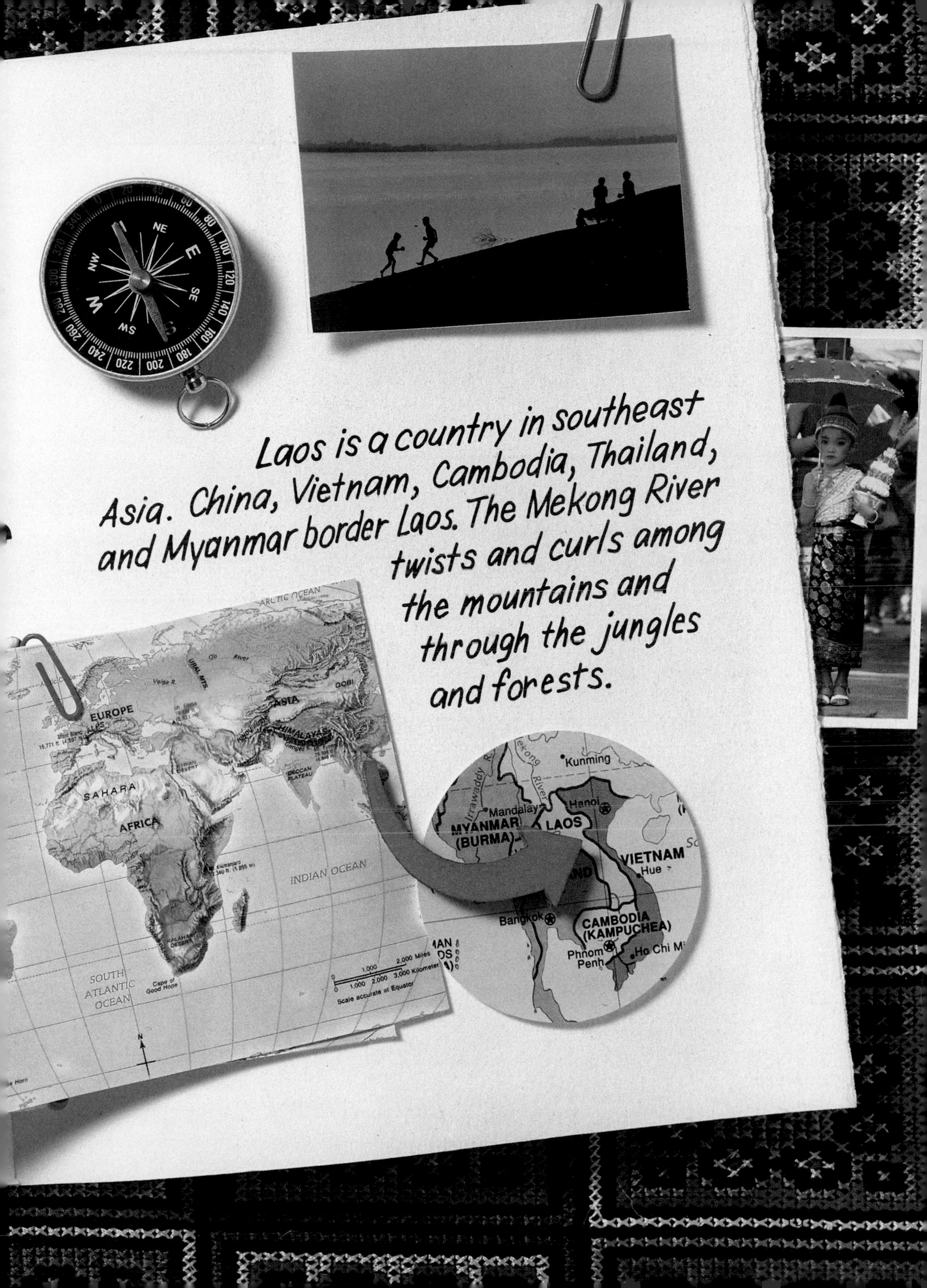


Laos is a country in southeast Asia. China, Vietnam, Cambodia, Thailand, and Myanmar border Laos. The Mekong River twists and curls among the mountains and through the jungles and forests.

# The Wednesday Surprise

*by Eve Bunting*

I like surprises. But the one Grandma and I are planning for Dad's birthday is the best surprise of all.

We work on it Wednesday nights. On Wednesdays Mom has to stay late at the office and my brother, Sam, goes to basketball practice at the Y. That's when Grandma rides the bus across town to stay with me.

I watch for her from the window and I blow on the glass to make breath pictures while I wait. When I see her I call: "Sam! She's here!" and he says it's okay to run down, down the long stairs and wait by the door.

"Grandma!" I call.

KLES

"Anna!" She's hurrying, her big, cloth bag bumping against her legs.

We meet and hug. She tells me how much I've grown since last week and I tell her how much she's grown, too, which is our joke. Between us we carry her lumpy bag upstairs.

I show Grandma my breath picture, if it's still there. Mostly she knows what it is. Mostly she's the only one who does.

On Wednesday nights we have hot dogs.

"Have you heard from your dad?" Grandma asks Sam.

"He'll be back Saturday, same as always," Sam says. "In time for his birthday."

"His birthday?" Grandma raises her eyebrows as if she'd forgotten all about that.

Grandma is some actress!

When Sam goes she and I do the dishes. Then we get down to business.

I sit beside her on the couch and she takes the first picture book from the bag. We read the story together, out loud, and when we finish one book we start a second.

We read for an hour, get some ice cream, then read some more.

Grandma gives me another hug. "Only seven years old and smart as paint already!"

I'm pleased. "They're all going to be so surprised on Saturday," I say.

When Sam comes home we play card games, and when Mom comes she plays, too.

"You'll be here for the birthday dinner?" Mom asks as Grandma is getting ready to leave.

"Oh yes, the birthday," Grandma says vaguely, as if she'd forgotten again. As if we hadn't been working on our special surprise for weeks and weeks. Grandma is tricky.

"I'll be here," she says.

Sam walks Grandma to the bus stop. As they're going down the stairs I hear him say: "What have you got in this bag, Grandma? Bricks?"

That makes me smile.

Dad comes home Saturday morning, and we rush at him with our *Happy Birthdays.* He has brought Sam a basketball magazine and me a pebble, smooth and speckled as an egg, for my rock collection.

"I found it in the desert, close to the truck stop," he says. "It was half covered with sand."

I hold it, imagining I can still feel the desert sun hot inside it. How long did it lie there? What kind of rock is it?

Dad has stopped to pick wildflowers for Mom. They're wilting and she runs to put them in water. Then Dad has to go to bed because he has been driving his big truck all through the night.

While Dad sleeps, Sam and I hang red and blue streamers in the living room. We help Mom frost the cake. We've made Dad's favorite dinner, pot roast, and our gifts are wrapped and ready.

I watch for Grandma and help carry the bag upstairs. Wow! Sam should feel how heavy it is now! Grandma has brought a ton of books. We hide the bag behind the couch. I am sick from being nervous.

Grandma usually has seconds but tonight she doesn't. I don't either. I can tell Mom is worried about the pot roast but Grandma tells her it's very good.

"Are you feeling well, Mama?" Dad asks Grandma. "How are your knees?"

"Fine. Fine. The knees are fine."

Dad blows out the birthday candles and we give him his gifts. Then Grandma shoots a glance in my direction and I go for the big bag and drag it across to the table. I settle it on the floor between us.

"Another present?" Dad asks.

"It's a special surprise for your birthday, Dad, from Grandma and me."

My heart's beating awfully fast as I unzip the bag and give the first book to Grandma. It's called *Popcorn.* I squeeze Grandma's hand and she stands and begins to read.

Mom and Dad and Sam are all astonished.

Dad jumps up and says: "What's this?" but Mom shushes him and pulls him back down.

Grandma has the floor. She finishes *Popcorn,* which takes quite a while, gives the book back to me and beams all over her face.

"My goodness!" Mom is beaming too. "When did this wonderful thing happen? When did you learn to read?"

"Anna taught me," Grandma says.

"On Wednesday nights," I add. "And she took the books home, and practiced."

"You were always telling me to go to classes, classes, classes," Grandma says to Dad. She looks at Mom. "You must learn to read, you say. So? I come to Anna."

I giggle because I'm so excited.

Grandma reads and acts out *The Easter Pig*. And *The Velveteen Rabbit*.

"It's much smarter if you learn to read when you're young," she tells Sam sternly. "The chance may pass along with the years."

Sam looks hurt. "But I *can* read, Grandma."

"Nevertheless." She takes out another book.

"Are you going to read everything in that bag, Mama?" Dad asks her. He's grinning, but his eyes are brimming over with tears and he and Mom are holding hands across the table.

"Maybe I will read everything in the world now that I've started," Grandma says in a stuck-up way. "I've got time." She winks at me.

"So, Anna? What do you think? Was it a good surprise?"

I run to her and she puts her cheek against mine. "The best ever," I say.

# *Meet* EVE BUNTING

There's a story about *The Wednesday Surprise,* and Eve Bunting tells about it like this: "A friend took me out to dinner and began talking about her mother, Katina, who was quite a character.

"She told a story about how she taught her mother to read English with her picture books. Every day she would bring books home from school or the library, and they would read them together. *The Wednesday Surprise* is my book, but it's Katina's story."

Ms. Bunting loves Donald Carrick's illustrations. She asked him if the kitchen in *The Wednesday Surprise* was like his kitchen. He said to her, "Oh, yes. There's always a bit of my house in my books."

# *Meet* DONALD CARRICK

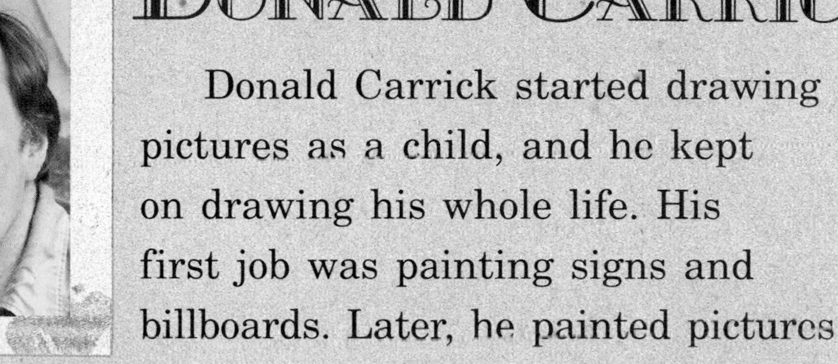

Donald Carrick started drawing pictures as a child, and he kept on drawing his whole life. His first job was painting signs and billboards. Later, he painted pictures for newspaper and magazine ads. His wife, Carol, wrote the first children's book he ever illustrated, *The Old Barn.* After that, Donald Carrick illustrated more than eighty picture books. Some of the most popular ones are about a boy named Christopher and his two dogs. Two other well-known books are about a boy named Patrick who imagines there are dinosaurs everywhere.

# WHAT in the WORLD?

**EVE MERRIAM**

What in the world
goes whiskery friskery
meowling and prowling
napping and lapping
at silky milk?
Psst
What is it?

What in the world
goes leaping and beeping
onto a lily pad onto a log
onto a tree stump or down to the bog?
Splash, blurp,
Kerchurp!

What in the world
goes gnawing and pawing
scratching and latching
sniffing and squiffing
nibbling for tidbits of left-over cheese?
Please?

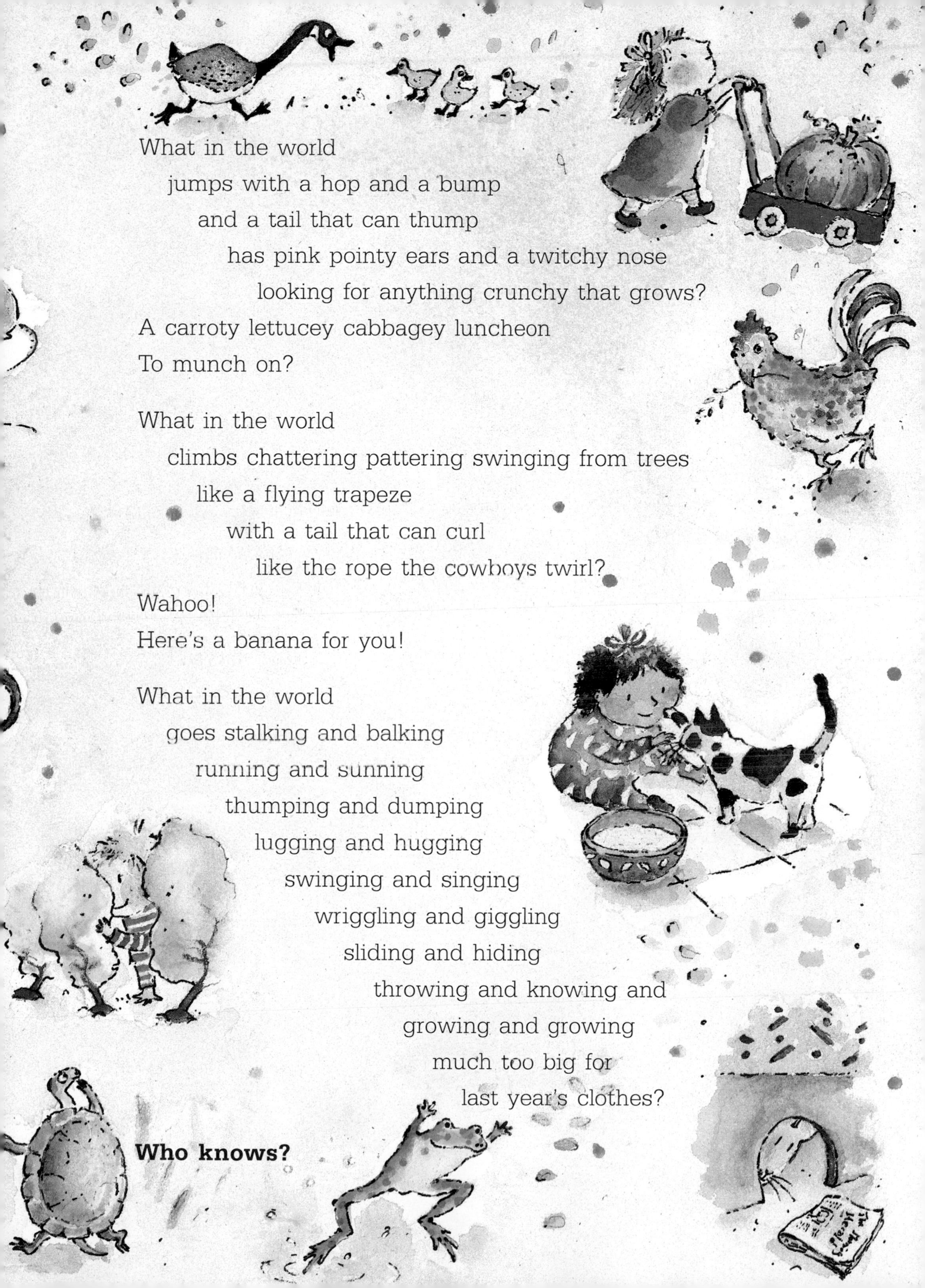

What in the world
jumps with a hop and a bump
and a tail that can thump
has pink pointy ears and a twitchy nose
looking for anything crunchy that grows?
A carroty lettucey cabbagey luncheon
To munch on?

What in the world
climbs chattering pattering swinging from trees
like a flying trapeze
with a tail that can curl
like the rope the cowboys twirl?
Wahoo!
Here's a banana for you!

What in the world
goes stalking and balking
running and sunning
thumping and dumping
lugging and hugging
swinging and singing
wriggling and giggling
sliding and hiding
throwing and knowing and
growing and growing
much too big for
last year's clothes?

**Who knows?**

## CONTENTS

UNIT

3

# TEAMING UP

The more we get
together, together,
together,

The more we get
together, the
happier we'll be!

from the German folk song
"The More We Get Together"

The
MYSTERIOUS
Tadpole
by Steven Kellogg

Uncle McAllister lived in Scotland.

Every year he sent Louis a birthday gift for his nature collection.

"This is the best one yet!" cried Louis.

The next day he took his entire collection to school for show-and-tell.

"Class, this is a tadpole," said Mrs. Shelbert. She asked Louis to bring it back often so they could all watch it become a frog.

Louis named the tadpole Alphonse. Every day Alphonse ate several cheeseburgers.

Louis found that he was eager to learn.

When Alphonse became too big for his jar, Louis moved him to the sink.

After Alphonse outgrew the sink, Louis's parents agreed to let him use the bathtub.

One day Mrs. Shelbert decided that Alphonse was not turning into an ordinary frog.

She asked Louis to stop bringing him to school.

By the time summer vacation arrived, Alphonse was enormous.

"He's too big for the bathtub," said Louis's mother.

"He's too big for the apartment," said Louis's father.

"He needs a swimming pool," said Louis.

"There is no place in our apartment for a swimming pool," said his parents.

Louis suggested that they buy the parking lot next door and build a swimming pool.

"It would cost more money than we have," said his parents. "Your tadpole will have to be donated to the zoo."

The thought of Alphonse in a cage made Louis very sad.

Then, in the middle of the night, Louis remembered that the junior high had a swimming pool that nobody used during the summer.

Louis hid Alphonse under a rug and smuggled him into the school.

After making sure that Alphonse felt at home, Louis went back to bed.

Every morning Louis spent several hours swimming with his friend. In the afternoon he earned the money for Alphonse's cheeseburgers by delivering newspapers.

Meanwhile the training continued. Alphonse learned to retrieve things from the bottom of the pool.

Summer vacation passed quickly. Louis worried what would happen to Alphonse now that school had reopened.

As soon as the first day ended, he ran to the junior high. The students were getting ready for after-school activities.

Louis arrived just as the first swimming race began.

Alphonse was delighted to see all the swimmers.

"It's a submarine from another planet!" bellowed the coach. "Call the police! Call the Navy!"

"No! It's a tadpole!" cried Louis. "He's my pet!"

The coach was upset and confused.

"You have until tomorrow," he cried, "to get that creature out of the pool!"

Louis didn't know what to do. On the way home he met his friend Miss Seevers, the librarian, and he told her his problem.

Miss Seevers went back to the junior high school with Louis, but when she saw Alphonse, she was so shocked that she dropped her purse and the books she was carrying into the swimming pool. Alphonse retrieved them.

Then Miss Seevers telephoned Louis's Uncle McAllister in Scotland. He told her that he had caught the little tadpole in Loch Ness, a large lake near his cottage.

Miss Seevers said, "I'm convinced that your uncle has given you a very rare Loch Ness monster!"

"I don't care!" cried Louis. "He's my pet, and I love him!" He begged Miss Seevers to help him raise enough money to buy the parking lot near his apartment so he could build a swimming pool for Alphonse.

Suddenly Miss Seevers had an idea.

"In 1639 there was a battle in our city's harbor," she said. "A pirate treasure ship was sunk, and no one has ever been able to find it. But perhaps we can!"

The next morning Miss Seevers and Louis rented a boat.

In the middle of the harbor Louis showed Alphonse a picture of a treasure chest.

Alphonse disappeared under the water.

Louis and Miss Seevers bought the parking lot.
THE SCAMPI BROTHERS PARKING LOT
They hired some helpers.
H and P
HUFF and PUFF CONSTRUCTION COMPANY
HUFF
PUFF

And when the pool was completed, all

the children in the city were invited to swim.

That night Louis said, "Alphonse, next week is my birthday, which means that we've been friends for almost a year."

Far away in Scotland Uncle McAllister was also thinking about the approaching birthday. While out hiking he discovered an unusual stone in a clump of grass and sticks.

"A perfect gift for my nephew!" he cried. "I'll deliver it in person!"

Uncle McAllister arrived at Louis's apartment and gave Louis the present.

Louis couldn't wait to add it to his collection.

Suddenly a crack appeared in the stone. . . .

When asked why he wrote *The Mysterious Tadpole,* Steven Kellogg said, "My parents weren't enthusiastic about having animals in the home. But I loved animals as a child, and I still do."

He added, "I have always been fascinated with the Loch Ness monster. I like it because it remains mysterious. I always wonder if there are young ones. Are they tadpoles?"

But Mr. Kellogg says this is not just a book about having a pet or the Loch Ness monster. He says, "This book is about friendship. Alphonse is unacceptable to the parents and the teacher, but not to Louis. Louis loves him so much that he tries to make his friend a part of his life."

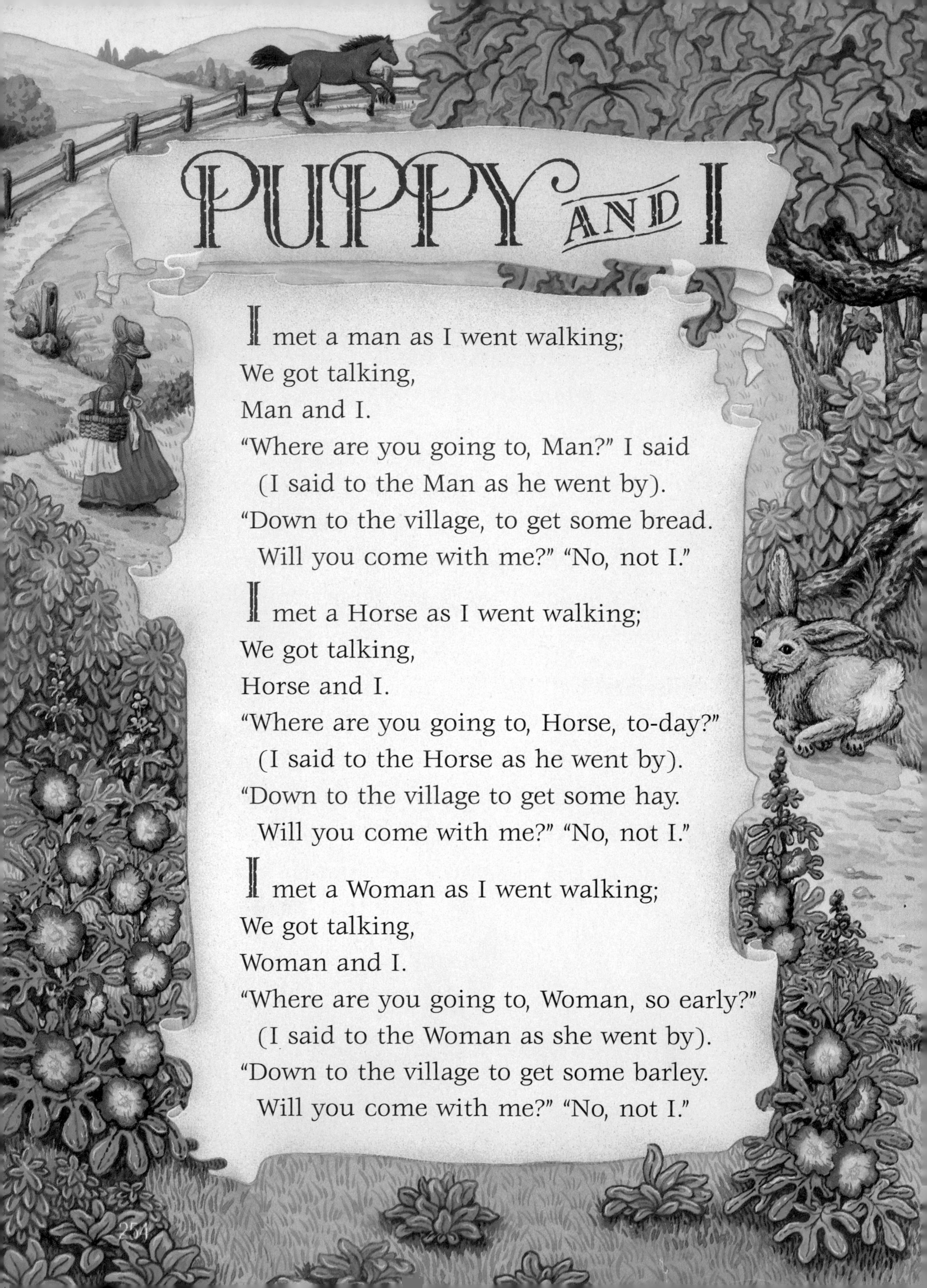

# PUPPY AND I

I met a man as I went walking;
We got talking,
Man and I.
"Where are you going to, Man?" I said
(I said to the Man as he went by).
"Down to the village, to get some bread.
Will you come with me?" "No, not I."

I met a Horse as I went walking;
We got talking,
Horse and I.
"Where are you going to, Horse, to-day?"
(I said to the Horse as he went by).
"Down to the village to get some hay.
Will you come with me?" "No, not I."

I met a Woman as I went walking;
We got talking,
Woman and I.
"Where are you going to, Woman, so early?"
(I said to the Woman as she went by).
"Down to the village to get some barley.
Will you come with me?" "No, not I."

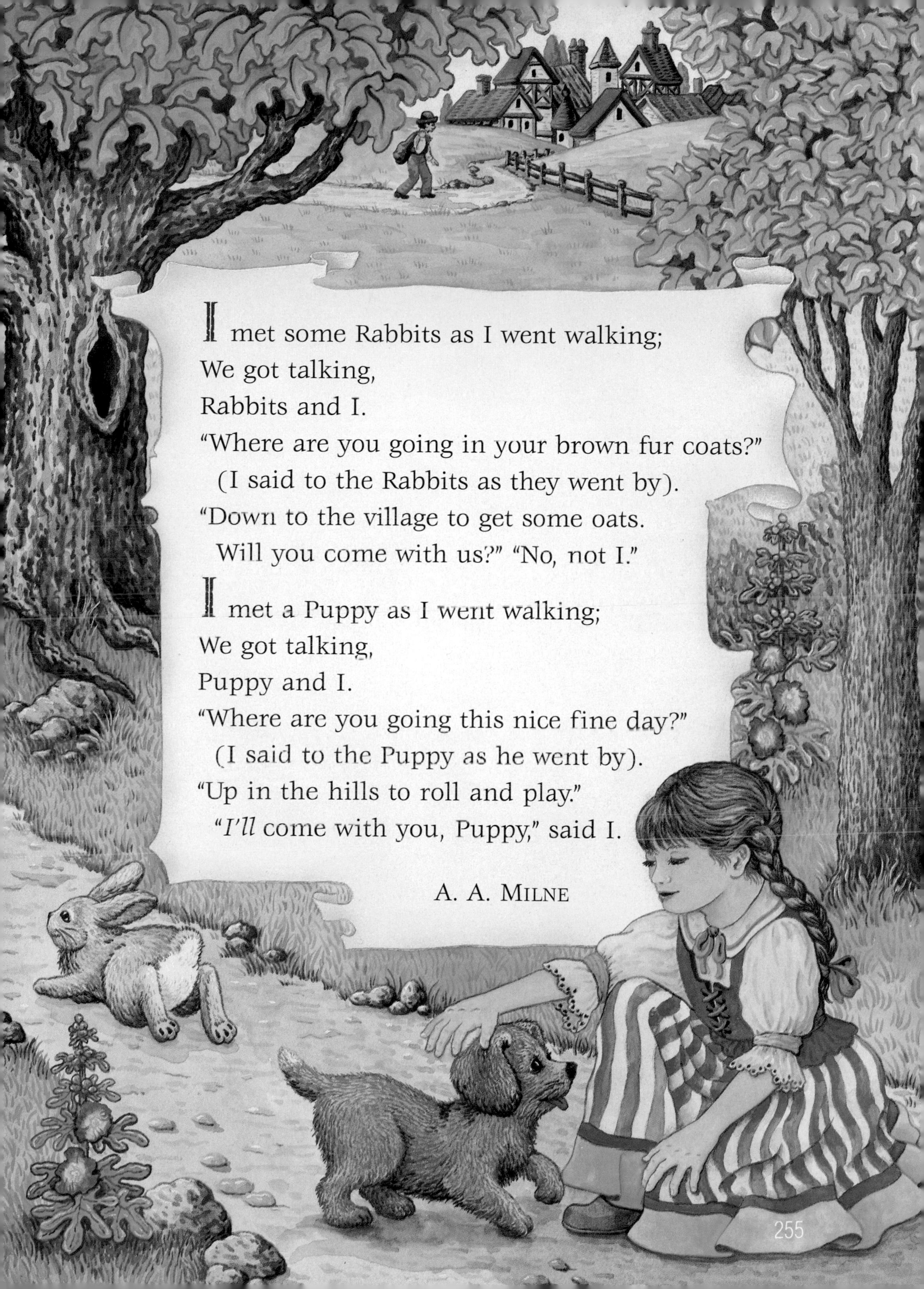

I met some Rabbits as I went walking;
We got talking,
Rabbits and I.
"Where are you going in your brown fur coats?"
(I said to the Rabbits as they went by).
"Down to the village to get some oats.
Will you come with us?" "No, not I."

I met a Puppy as I went walking;
We got talking,
Puppy and I.
"Where are you going this nice fine day?"
(I said to the Puppy as he went by).
"Up in the hills to roll and play."
"*I'll* come with you, Puppy," said I.

A. A. MILNE

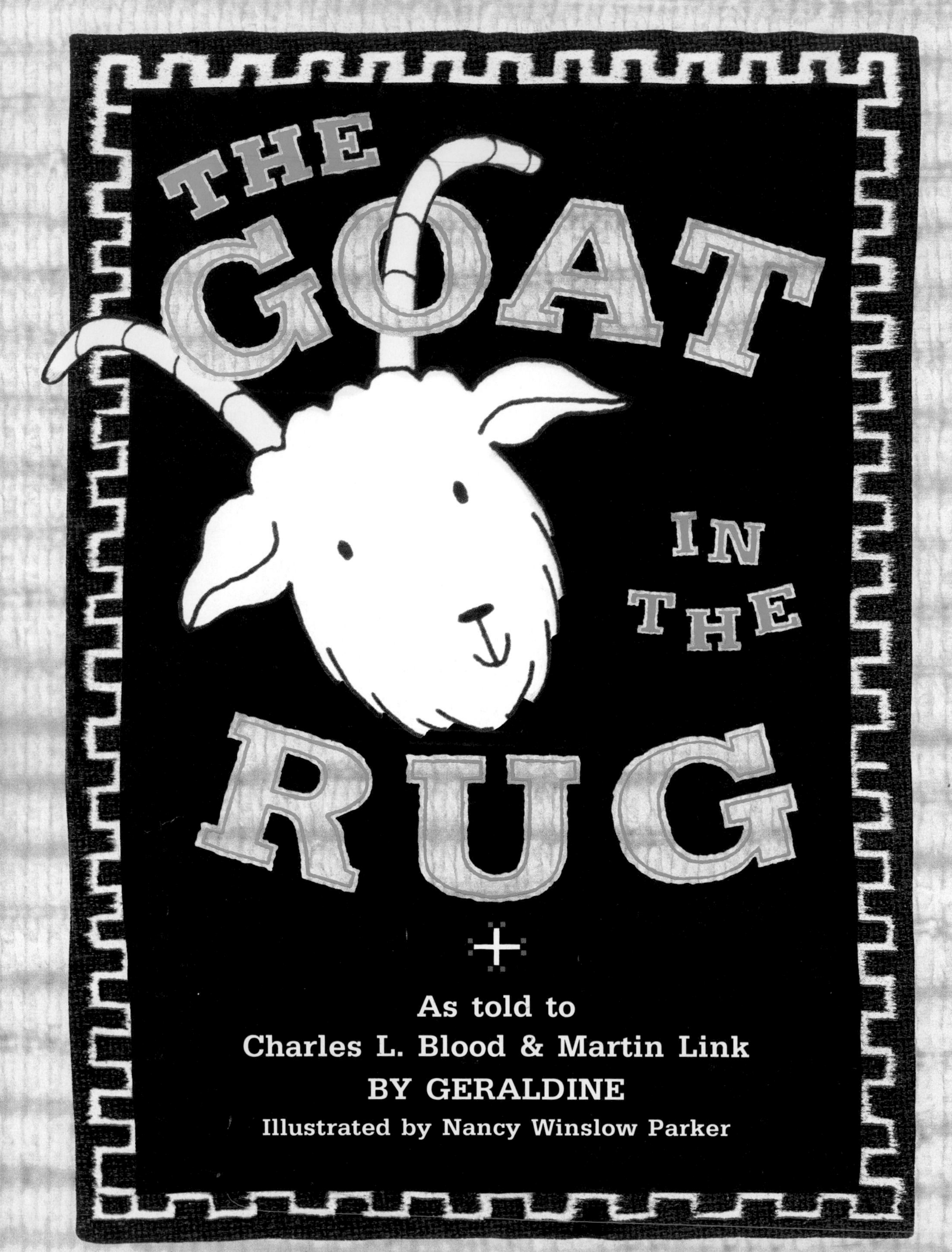
THE GOAT IN THE RUG
As told to
Charles L. Blood & Martin Link
BY GERALDINE
Illustrated by Nancy Winslow Parker

My name is Geraldine and I live near a place called Window Rock with my Navajo friend, Glenmae. It's called Window Rock because it has a big round hole in it that looks like a window open to the sky.

Glenmae is called Glenmae most of the time because it's easier to say than her Indian name: Glee 'Nasbah. In English that means something like female warrior, but she's really a Navajo weaver. I guess that's why, one day, she decided to weave me into a rug.

I remember it was a warm, sunny afternoon. Glenmae had spent most of the morning sharpening a large pair of scissors. I had no idea what she was going to use them for, but it didn't take me long to find out.

Before I knew what was happening, I was on the ground and Glenmae was clipping off my wool in great long strands. (It's called mohair, really.) It didn't hurt at all, but I admit I kicked up my heels some. I'm very ticklish for a goat.

**I** might have looked a little naked and silly afterwards, but my, did I feel nice and cool! So I decided to stick around and see what would happen next.

The first thing Glenmae did was chop up roots from a yucca plant. The roots made a soapy, rich lather when she mixed them with water.

She washed my wool in the suds until it was clean and white.

After that, a little bit of me (you might say) was hung up in the sun to dry. When my wool was dry, Glenmae took out two large square combs with many teeth.

By combing my wool between these carding combs, as they're called, she removed any bits of twigs or burrs and straightened out the fibers. She told me it helped make a smoother yarn for spinning.

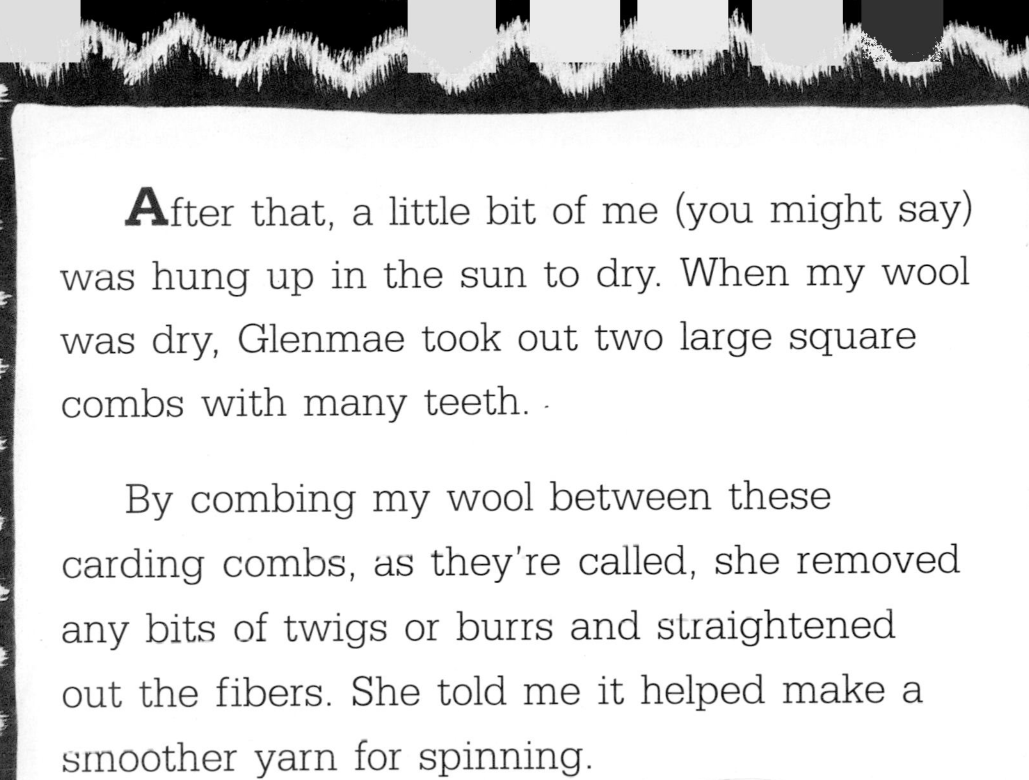

Then, Glenmae carefully started to spin my wool—one small bundle at a time—into yarn. I was beginning to find out it takes a long while to make a Navajo rug.

Again and again, Glenmae twisted and pulled, twisted and pulled the wool. Then she spun it around a long, thin stick she called a spindle. As she twisted and pulled and spun, the finer, stronger and smoother the yarn became.

**A** few days later, Glenmae and I went for a walk. She said we were going to find some special plants she would use to make dye.

I didn't know what "dye" meant, but it sounded like a picnic to me. I do love to eat plants. That's what got me into trouble.

While Glenmae was out looking for more plants, I ate every one she had already collected in her bucket. Delicious!

The next day, Glenmae made me stay home while she walked miles to a store. She said the dye she could buy wasn't the same as the kind she makes from plants, but since I'd made such a pig of myself, it would have to do.

**I** was really worried that she would still be angry with me when she got back. She wasn't, though, and pretty soon she had three big potfuls of dye boiling over a fire.

Then I saw what Glenmae had meant by dyeing. She dipped my white wool into one pot . . . and it turned pink! She dipped it in again. It turned a darker pink! By the time she'd finished dipping it in and out and hung it up to dry, it was a beautiful deep red.

After that, she dyed some of my wool brown, and some of it black. I couldn't help wondering if those plants I'd eaten would turn all of me the same colors.

While I was worrying about that, Glenmae started to make our rug. She took a ball of yarn and wrapped it around and around two poles. I lost count when she'd reached three hundred wraps. I guess I was too busy thinking about what it would be like to be the only red, white, black and brown goat at Window Rock.

It wasn't long before Glenmae had finished wrapping. Then she hung the poles with the yarn on a big wooden frame. It looked like a picture frame made of logs—she called it a "loom."

After a whole week of getting ready to weave, Glenmae started. She began weaving at the bottom of the loom. Then, one strand of yarn at a time, our rug started growing toward the top.

**A** few strands of black.

A few of brown.

A few of red.

In and out. Back and forth.

Until, in a few days, the pattern of our rug was clear to see.

Our rug grew very slowly. Just as every Navajo weaver before her had done for hundreds and hundreds of years, Glenmae formed a design that would never be duplicated.

Then, at last, the weaving was finished! But not until I'd checked it quite thoroughly in front . . .

. . . and in back, did I let Glenmae take our rug off the loom.

There was a lot of me in that rug. I wanted it to be perfect. And it was.

Since then, my wool has grown almost long enough for Glenmae and me to make another rug. I hope we do very soon. Because, you see, there aren't too many weavers like Glenmae left among the Navajos.

And there's only one goat like me, Geraldine.

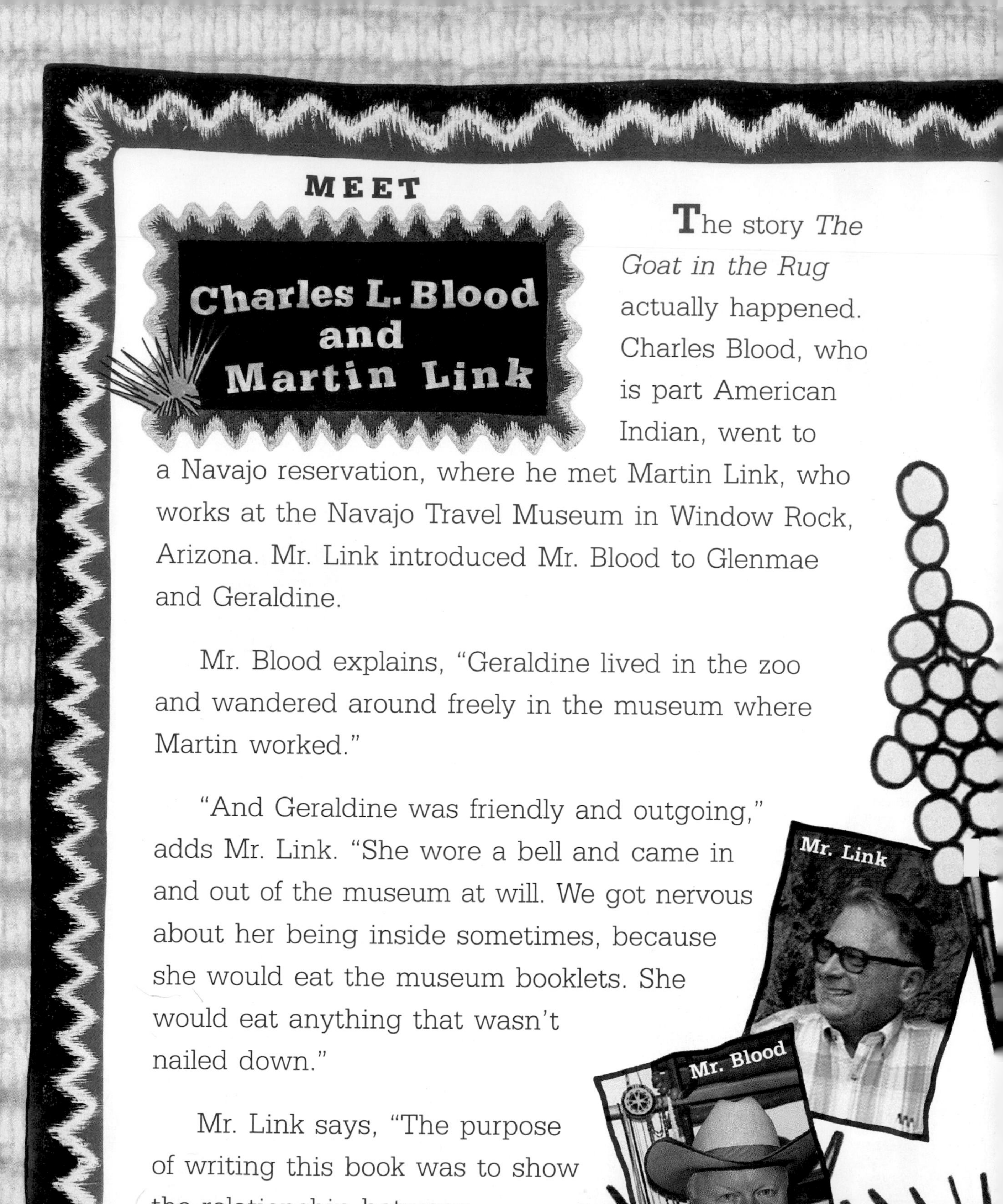


MEET

# Charles L. Blood and Martin Link

The story *The Goat in the Rug* actually happened. Charles Blood, who is part American Indian, went to a Navajo reservation, where he met Martin Link, who works at the Navajo Travel Museum in Window Rock, Arizona. Mr. Link introduced Mr. Blood to Glenmae and Geraldine.

Mr. Blood explains, "Geraldine lived in the zoo and wandered around freely in the museum where Martin worked."

"And Geraldine was friendly and outgoing," adds Mr. Link. "She wore a bell and came in and out of the museum at will. We got nervous about her being inside sometimes, because she would eat the museum booklets. She would eat anything that wasn't nailed down."

Mr. Link says, "The purpose of writing this book was to show the relationship between Native American culture

and the animal world. Native Americans know how to live in harmony and cooperation with the animals. They can teach us how to do this."

## MEET Nancy Winslow Parker

"When I first saw *The Goat in the Rug*, I knew I wanted to draw pictures for it," said Nancy Winslow Parker. "I spent a lot of time looking at exhibits in museums to find out about the Navajos. I also read a lot of books about weaving and studied Navajo rugs and clothes. I used what I learned to make the border designs and the clothes Glenmae wears."

The authors also helped Ms. Parker. "Mr. Link and Mr. Blood gave me photographs of a weaver on a Navajo reservation in Window Rock," she explains. "The photographs helped me a lot."

# My Horse, Fly Like a Bird

My horse, fly like a bird
To carry me far
From the arrows of my enemies,
And I will tie red ribbons
To your streaming hair.

*Virginia Driving Hawk Sneve*
*adapted from*
*a Lakota warrior's*
*song to his horse*

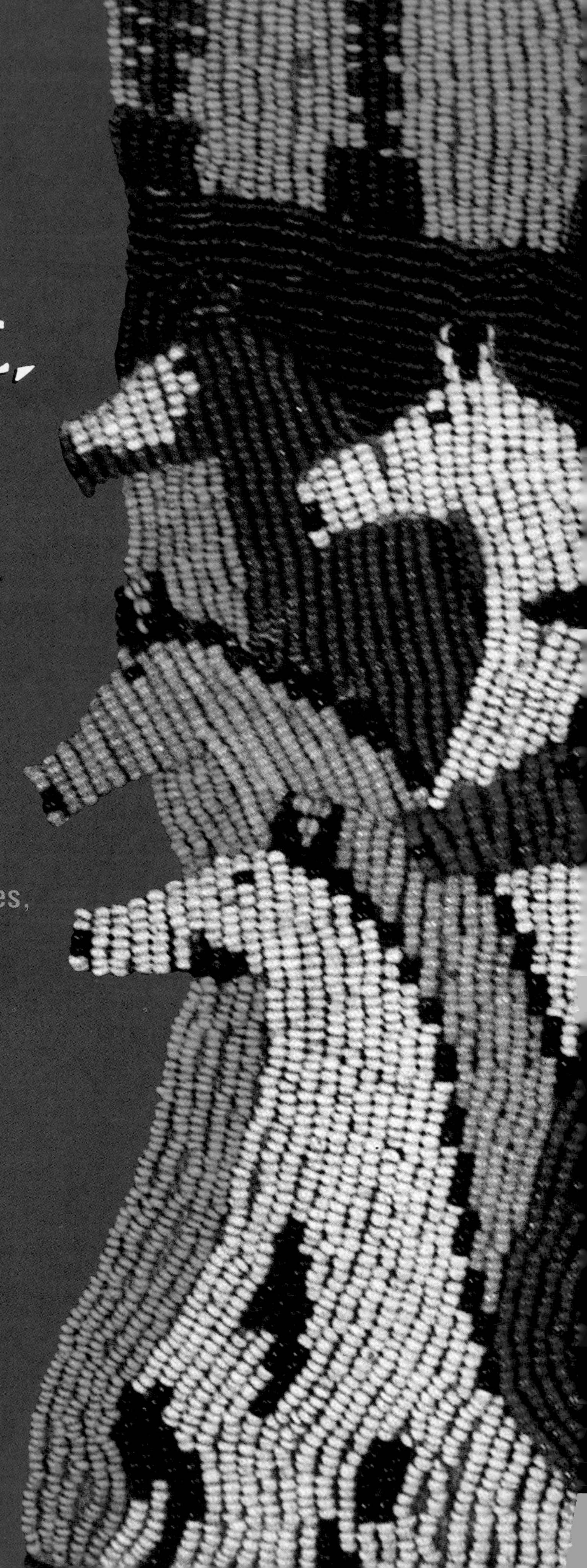

This photograph shows part of a beaded bag made by a Cheyenne River Sioux, somewhere between the years 1885 and 1890. The beads are sewn on a hide and show the Miniconjou chief White Swan.

# In the Animal Kingdom

**Young Lions**

Written and illustrated by Toshi Yoshida

Philomel Books, 1989

But three young lions are restless.

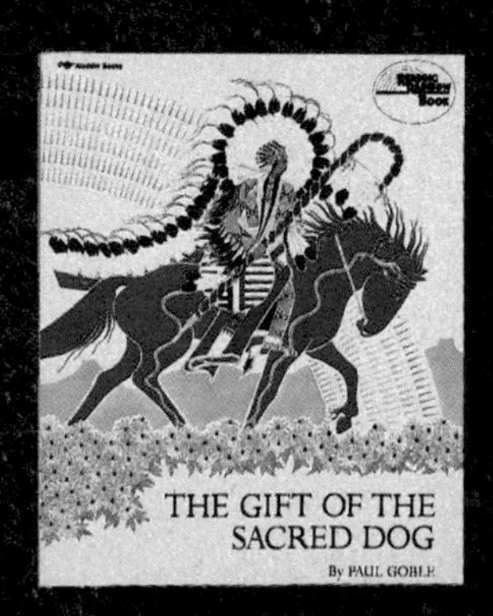


**The Gift of the Sacred Dog**

Written and illustrated by Paul Goble

Bradbury Press, 1980

The four winds are blowing;
some horses are coming.

# HENRY'S

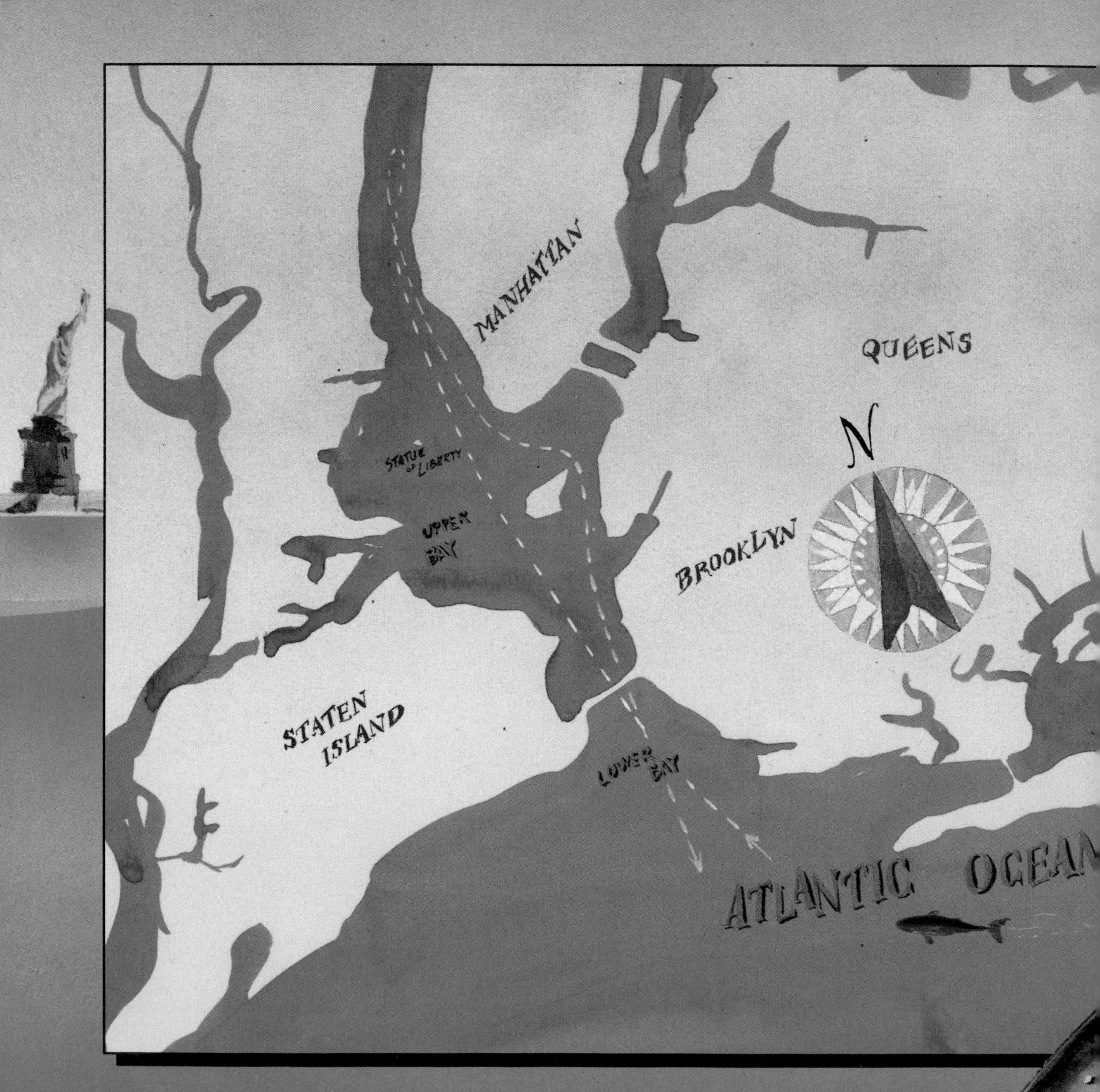

MANHATTAN
QUEENS
N
STATUE OF LIBERTY
UPPER BAY
BROOKLYN
STATEN ISLAND
LOWER BAY
ATLANTIC OCEAN

# WRONG TURN

WRITTEN BY
HARRIET ZIEFERT

ILLUSTRATED BY
ANDREA BARUFFI

LONG ISLAND

He was a big humpback whale who made a wrong turn. He was swimming in the ocean, and instead of going out to sea, he turned and went up the Hudson River—right into New York Harbor.

No one knew why Henry—for that is what someone named him—wanted to be in New York Harbor. Certainly there was nothing for him to eat in those waters. But there he was.

Henry swam under the Verrazano-Narrows Bridge. The day was bright and sunny, and on the bridge, traffic moved right along. No one up there noticed Henry, but down in the harbor, a tugboat captain did. He signaled to all the other boats: *Watch out for the whale!*

There was lots of excitement. No one could remember seeing a whale in New York Harbor. Everyone was on the lookout for Henry. But where was he?

"Look! There he is!" shouted one of the visitors to the Statue of Liberty. "Take a good look, everyone, because you probably won't see another one like him again."

Queen Elizabeth 2

The *Queen Elizabeth 2* passed Henry on her way to sea. He was quite small next to the mighty liner. The ship sounded its horn and Henry again dove under the water.

The Coast Guard wanted to help Henry, so they sent a boat to follow him.

Henry quickly swam away from the patrol boat. He passed an aircraft carrier, *Intrepid.* Visitors on deck cheered when Henry sent up a magnificent spray.

Suddenly, Henry disappeared.

No one saw Henry until evening. By then he was near the World Trade Center. He seemed lost. "We've got to help Henry go back to the ocean," the Coast Guard sailors told each other. "There are too many boats in the harbor. He could get hit!"

In the twilight, Henry headed past the Battery into Buttermilk Channel between Governors Island and Red Hook in Brooklyn.

Two ferries carrying commuters were just leaving their slips. The ferries immediately put their engines in reverse, veered off their courses and . . . avoided a collision with Henry!

COAST GUARD

Now the Coast Guard was back on Henry's tail. The captain of the cutter was determined to make him turn around and return to the ocean.

And it worked! Perhaps Henry didn't like the noise from the boat's engines. Perhaps he was hungry. For whatever reason, Henry turned around.

Henry swam fast. By the time the moon was in the sky, he was back at the Verrazano-Narrows Bridge, heading out to sea.

Henry left the
harbor, then he dove.
"Good luck, Henry!"

# Meet Harriet Ziefert and Andrea Baruffi

***Harriet Ziefert*** got the idea for *Henry's Wrong Turn* when she read about Henry, the whale, in the New York newspapers.

Harriet Ziefert decided not to make up what Henry was thinking and feeling. "We don't know why whales sometimes do what Henry did," she says. "We just know that sometimes they get confused."

Ms. Ziefert has written more than a hundred books for children. She tells children, "The more you write, the easier it becomes to write stories."

***Andrea Baruffi*** came to the United States from Italy. He says, "*Henry's Wrong Turn* was an exciting book for me because I was painting something that really happened. I live on the Hudson River where the story happened."

For this book, it was important for Mr. Baruffi to show New York Harbor. "One day I took a trip on a boat to see how I should paint the ferries," he says.

A humpback whale that swims in the Pacific Ocean spends its summer off the coast of Alaska. It travels to the waters of Hawaii, a journey of about 3,000 miles (4,827 kilometers), or Mexico, a journey of about 3,381 miles (5,440 kilometers), for the winter.

A humpback whale that swims in the Atlantic Ocean feeds during the summer near Maine, Canada, Greenland, or Iceland. In the winter, it travels to Puerto Rico or the tip of South America, a journey of about 11,433 miles (18,396 kilometers).

Greenland
Iceland
Alaska
Canada
Maine
ATLANTIC OCEAN
North America
Hawaii
Mexico
Puerto Rico
PACIFIC OCEAN
South America

Today, there are about 10,000 humpback whales. A hundred years ago, before hunters killed many of them, there were ten times that number. Now, laws protect humpback whales from hunters.

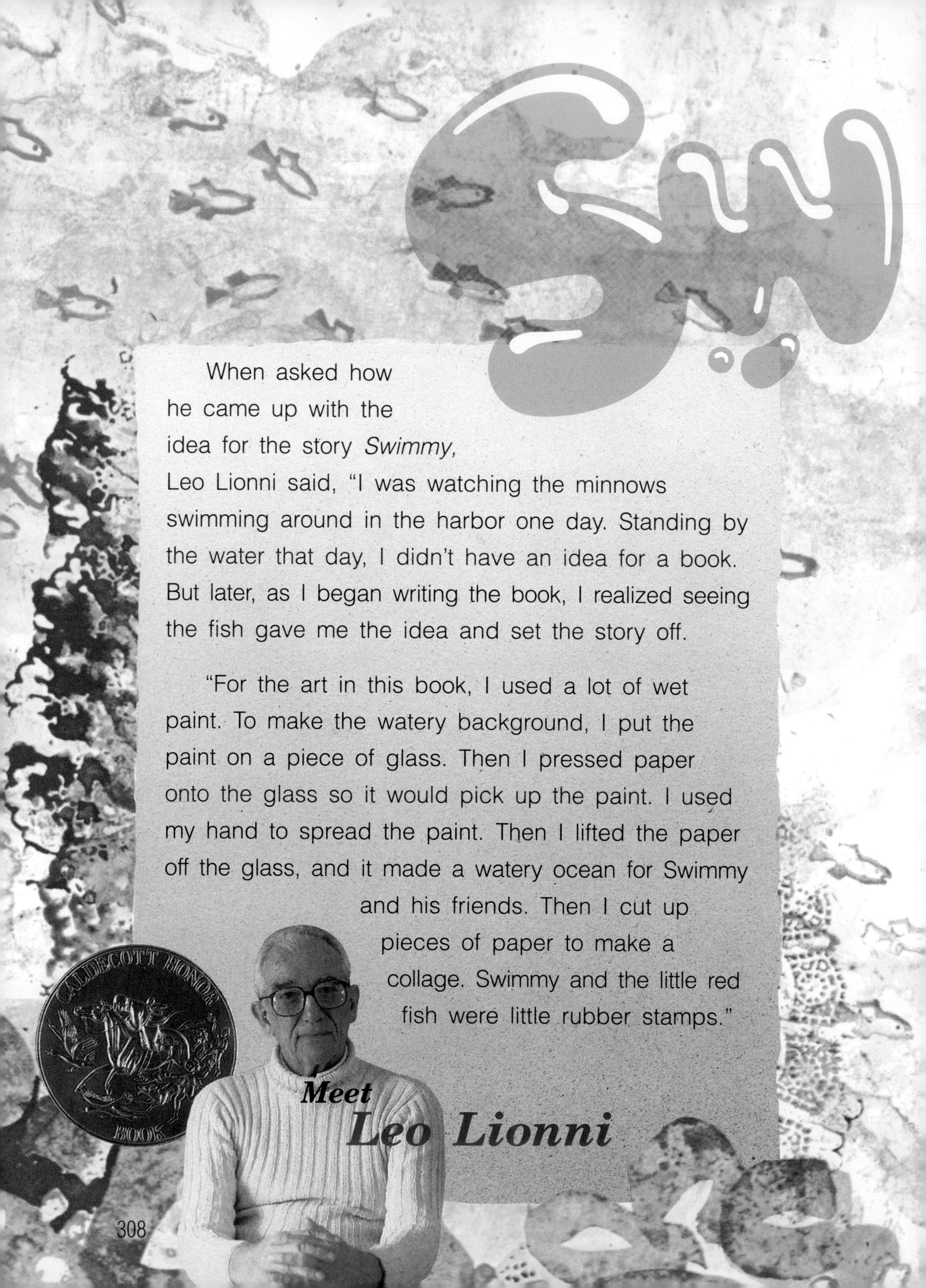


When asked how he came up with the idea for the story *Swimmy*, Leo Lionni said, "I was watching the minnows swimming around in the harbor one day. Standing by the water that day, I didn't have an idea for a book. But later, as I began writing the book, I realized seeing the fish gave me the idea and set the story off.

"For the art in this book, I used a lot of wet paint. To make the watery background, I put the paint on a piece of glass. Then I pressed paper onto the glass so it would pick up the paint. I used my hand to spread the paint. Then I lifted the paper off the glass, and it made a watery ocean for Swimmy and his friends. Then I cut up pieces of paper to make a collage. Swimmy and the little red fish were little rubber stamps."

## Meet Leo Lionni

# immy

*by Leo Lionni*

A happy school of little fish lived in a corner of the sea somewhere. They were all red. Only one of them was as black as a mussel shell. He swam faster than his brothers and sisters. His name was Swimmy.

One bad day a tuna fish, swift, fierce and very hungry, came darting through the waves. In one gulp he swallowed all the little red fish.

Only Swimmy escaped. He swam away in the deep wet world. He was scared, lonely and very sad.

But the sea was full of wonderful creatures, and as he swam from marvel to marvel Swimmy was happy again.

He saw a medusa made of rainbow jelly . . .

a lobster, who walked about like a water-moving machine . . .

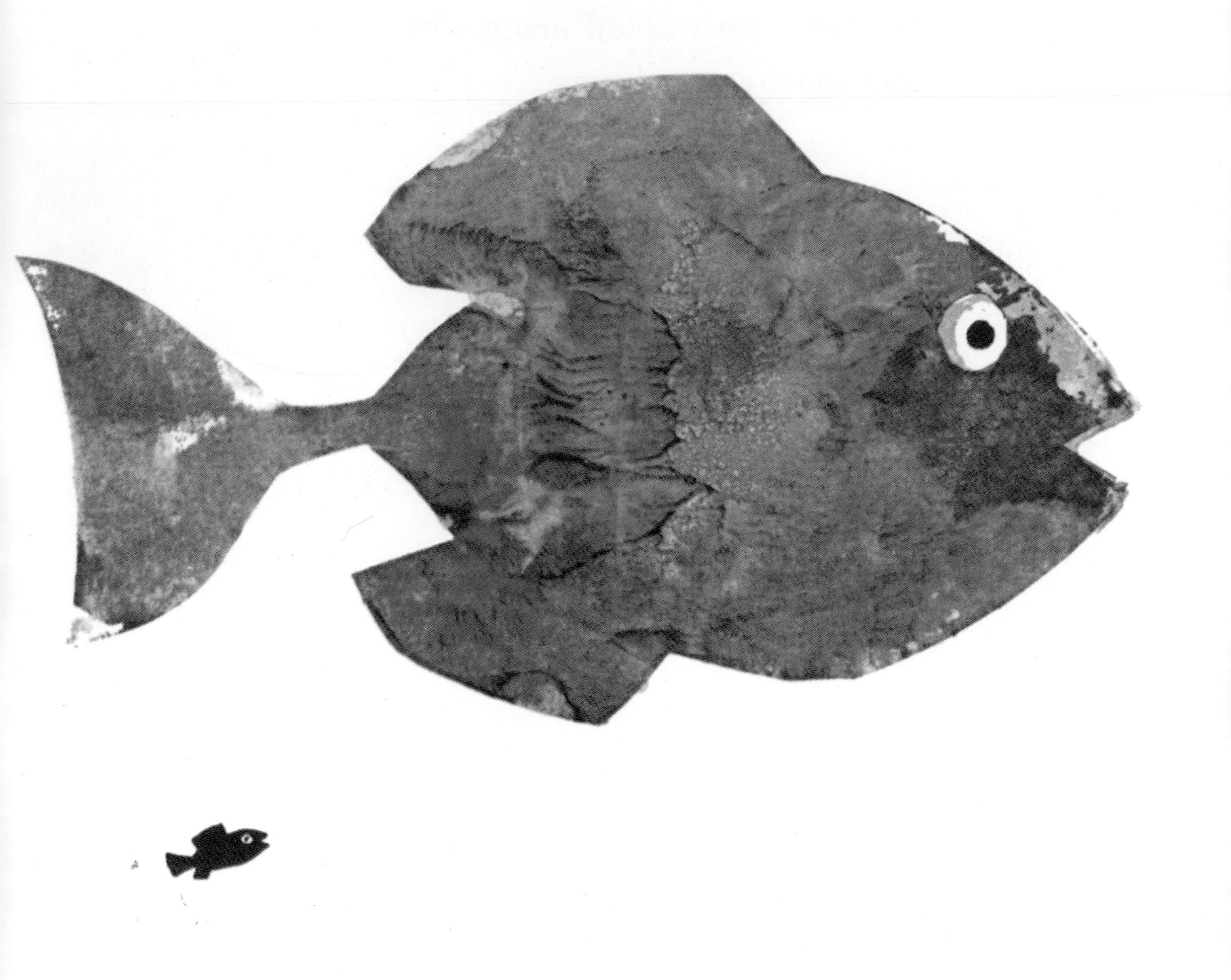

strange fish, pulled by an invisible thread . . .

a forest of seaweeds growing from
sugar-candy rocks . . .

an eel whose tail was almost too
far away to remember . . .

and sea anemones, who looked
like pink palm trees swaying
in the wind.

Then, hidden in the dark shade of rocks and weeds, he saw a school of little fish, just like his own.

"Let's go and swim and play and SEE things!" he said happily.

"We can't," said the little red fish. "The big fish will eat us all."

"But you can't just lie there," said Swimmy. "We must THINK of something."

Swimmy thought and thought and thought. Then suddenly he said, "I have it! We are going to swim all together like the biggest fish in the sea!"

He taught them to swim close together, each in his own place, and when they had learned to swim like one giant fish, he said, "I'll be the eye."

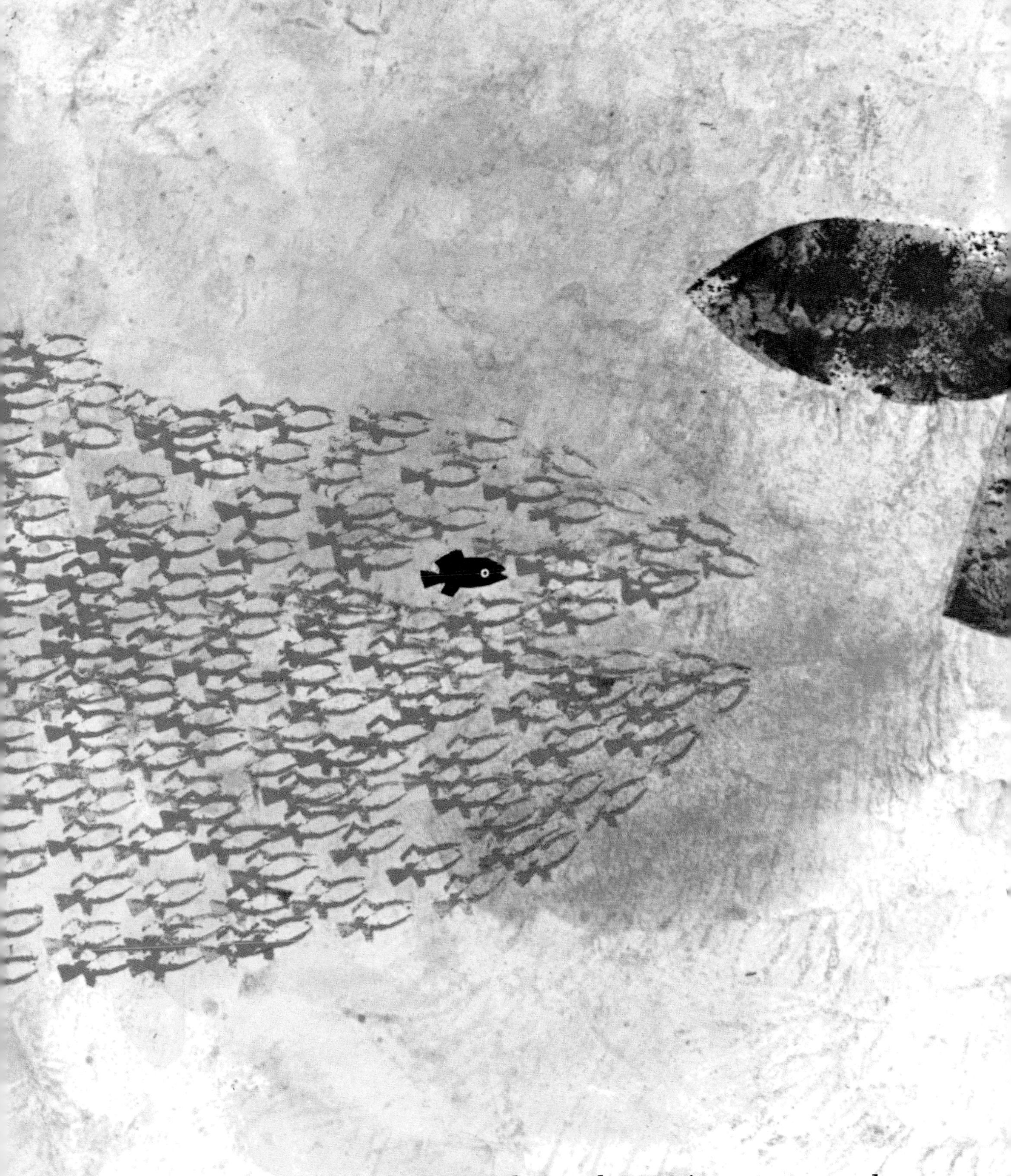

And so they swam in the cool morning water and in the midday sun and chased the big fish away.

# The Light-House-Keeper's White-Mouse

by John Ciardi

As I rowed out to the light-house
For a cup of tea one day,
I came on a very wet white-mouse
Out swimming in the bay.

"If you are for the light-house,"
Said he, "I'm glad we met.
I'm the light-house-keeper's white-mouse
And I fear I'm getting wet."

"O light-house-keeper's white-mouse,
I am rowing out for tea
With the keeper in his light-house.
Let me pull you in with me."

So I gave an oar to the white-mouse.
And I pulled on the other.
And we all had tea at the light-house
With the keeper and his mother.

Information Illustrated
A Guide To Skills And Information Sources That Go With The Stories You Are Reading!

CONTENTS

# Book Parts

## TITLE PAGE

HENRY AND MUDGE
AND THE
Bedtime Thumps

*The Ninth Book of Their Adventures*

Story by Cynthia Rylant
Pictures by Suçie Stevenson

BRADBURY PRESS • NEW YORK

Collier Macmillan Canada • Toronto
Maxwell Macmillan International Publishing Group
New York • Oxford • Singapore • Sydney

## TABLE OF CONTENTS

Contents

# INDEX

# Calendar 1993

## JANUARY

| SUN | MON | TUE | WED | THUR | FRI | SAT |
|---|---|---|---|---|---|---|
| | | | | | 1 | 2 |
| 3 | 4 | 5 | 6 | 7 | 8 | 9 |
| 10 | 11 | 12 | 13 | 14 | 15 | 16 |
| 17 | 18 | 19 | 20 | 21 | 22 | 23 |
| 24/31 | 25 | 26 | 27 | 28 | 29 | 30 |

## FEBRUARY

| SUN | MON | TUE | WED | THUR | FRI | SAT |
|---|---|---|---|---|---|---|
| | 1 | 2 | 3 | 4 | 5 | 6 |
| 7 | 8 | 9 | 10 | 11 | 12 | 13 |
| 14 | 15 | 16 | 17 | 18 | 19 | 20 |
| 21 | 22 | 23 | 24 | 25 | 26 | 27 |
| 28 | | | | | | |

## MARCH

| SUN | MON | TUE | WED | THUR | FRI | SAT |
|---|---|---|---|---|---|---|
| | 1 | 2 | 3 | 4 | 5 | 6 |
| 7 | 8 | 9 | 10 | 11 | 12 | 13 |
| 14 | 15 | 16 | 17 | 18 | 19 | 20 |
| 21 | 22 | 23 | 24 | 25 | 26 | 27 |
| 28 | 29 | 30 | 31 | | | |

## JULY

| SUN | MON | TUE | WED | THUR | FRI | SAT |
|---|---|---|---|---|---|---|
| | | | | 1 | 2 | 3 |
| 4 | 5 | 6 | 7 | 8 | 9 | 10 |
| 11 | 12 | 13 | 14 | 15 | 16 | 17 |
| 18 | 19 | 20 | 21 | 22 | 23 | 24 |
| 25 | 26 | 27 | 28 | 29 | 30 | 31 |

## APRIL

| SUN | MON | TUE | WED | THUR | FRI | SAT |
|---|---|---|---|---|---|---|
| | | | | 1 | 2 | 3 |
| 4 | 5 | 6 | 7 | 8 | 9 | 10 |
| 11 | 12 | 13 | 14 | 15 | 16 | 17 |
| 18 | 19 | 20 | 21 | 22 | 23 | 24 |
| 25 | 26 | 27 | 28 | 29 | 30 | |

## MAY

| SUN | MON | TUE | WED | THUR | FRI | SAT |
|---|---|---|---|---|---|---|
| | | | | | | 1 |
| 2 | 3 | 4 | 5 | 6 | 7 | 8 |
| 9 | 10 | 11 | 12 | 13 | 14 | 15 |
| 16 | 17 | 18 | 19 | 20 | 21 | 22 |
| 23/30 | 24/31 | 25 | 26 | 27 | 28 | 29 |

## JUNE

| SUN | MON | TUE | WED | THUR | FRI | SAT |
|---|---|---|---|---|---|---|
| | | 1 | 2 | 3 | 4 | 5 |
| 6 | 7 | 8 | 9 | 10 | 11 | 12 |
| 13 | 14 | 15 | 16 | 17 | 18 | 19 |
| 20 | 21 | 22 | 23 | 24 | 25 | 26 |
| 27 | 28 | 29 | 30 | | | |

## JULY

| SUN | MON | TUE | WED | THUR | FRI | SAT |
|---|---|---|---|---|---|---|
| | | | | 1 | 2 | 3 |
| 4 | 5 | 6 | 7 | 8 | 9 | 10 |
| 11 | 12 | 13 | 14 | 15 | 16 | 17 |
| 18 | 19 | 20 | 21 | 22 | 23 | 24 |
| 25 | 26 | 27 | 28 | 29 | 30 | 31 |

## AUGUST

| SUN | MON | TUE | WED | THUR | FRI | SAT |
|---|---|---|---|---|---|---|
| 1 | 2 | 3 | 4 | 5 | 6 | 7 |
| 8 | 9 | 10 | 11 | 12 | 13 | 14 |
| 15 | 16 | 17 | 18 | 19 | 20 | 21 |
| 22 | 23 | 24 | 25 | 26 | 27 | 28 |
| 29 | 30 | 31 | | | | |

## SEPTEMBER

| SUN | MON | TUE | WED | THUR | FRI | SAT |
|---|---|---|---|---|---|---|
| | | | 1 | 2 | 3 | 4 |
| 5 | 6 | 7 | 8 | 9 | 10 | 11 |
| 12 | 13 | 14 | 15 | 16 | 17 | 18 |
| 19 | 20 | 21 | 22 | 23 | 24 | 25 |
| 26 | 27 | 28 | 29 | 30 | | |

## OCTOBER

| SUN | MON | TUE | WED | THUR | FRI | SAT |
|---|---|---|---|---|---|---|
| | | | | | 1 | 2 |
| 3 | 4 | 5 | 6 | 7 | 8 | 9 |
| 10 | 11 | 12 | 13 | 14 | 15 | 16 |
| 17 | 18 | 19 | 20 | 21 | 22 | 23 |
| 24/31 | 25 | 26 | 27 | 28 | 29 | 30 |

## NOVEMBER

| SUN | MON | TUE | WED | THUR | FRI | SAT |
|---|---|---|---|---|---|---|
| | 1 | 2 | 3 | 4 | 5 | 6 |
| 7 | 8 | 9 | 10 | 11 | 12 | 13 |
| 14 | 15 | 16 | 17 | 18 | 19 | 20 |
| 21 | 22 | 23 | 24 | 25 | 26 | 27 |
| 28 | 29 | 30 | | | | |

## DECEMBER

| SUN | MON | TUE | WED | THUR | FRI | SAT |
|---|---|---|---|---|---|---|
| | | | 1 | 2 | 3 | 4 |
| 5 | 6 | 7 | 8 | 9 | 10 | 11 |
| 12 | 13 | 14 | 15 | 16 | 17 | 18 |
| 19 | 20 | 21 | 22 | 23 | 24 | 25 |
| 26 | 27 | 28 | 29 | 30 | 31 | |

# Dictionary

**Main Entry**

**Definition**

**Illustration**

**Caption**

**Plural**



## permit

**Permit** means to allow someone to do something. My parents will not **permit** my sister and me to play outside after it is dark. ▲ **permitted, permitting.**

## person

A **person** is a man, woman, or child. Fifty people can ride on the bus, but only one **person** can drive it. ▲ **persons.**

The veterinarian will see many kinds of **pets** today.

## pet

A **pet** is an animal that people care for in their homes. Dogs and cats are **pets.** Helen has two parakeets as **pets.** ▲ **pets.**

## petal

A **petal** is a part of a flower. The **petals** of a daisy are narrow and white or yellow. ▲ **petals.**

## pharmacy

A **pharmacy** is a store where drugs and medicines are sold. Another name for **pharmacy** is **drugstore.** ▲ **pharmacies.**

248

# Dictionary

Guide Words

phone / picture

## phone

1. **Phone** is a short word for **telephone.** The Colemans have three **phones** in their house. ▲ **phones.**
2. **Phone** means to use a telephone. We **phoned** my aunt tonight to sing "Happy Birthday" to her. ▲ **phoned, phoning.**

Photograph

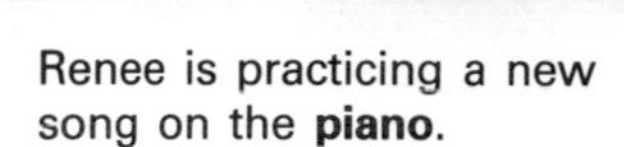

Renee is practicing a new song on the **piano**.

## photograph

A **photograph** is a picture that you take with a camera. Polly took a **photograph** of our class. ▲ **photographs.**

## piano

A **piano** is something that makes music. **Pianos** have black and white keys that you play with your fingers. Ian practices the **piano** every day for his concert. ▲ **pianos.**

Example Sentence

## pick

1. **Pick** means to take something in your hand. We're going to **pick** some flowers for Dad's birthday. The children **picked** up their toys and put them away.
2. **Pick** also means to choose something. Mom helped me **pick** a dress to wear to the party. ▲ **picked, picking.**

Verb Forms

Kim and Angela are **picking** flowers for their new neighbor.

## picnic

When you go on a **picnic,** you take food with you to eat outdoors. We brought sandwiches and fruit for a **picnic.** ▲ **picnics.**

## picture

A **picture** is something that you draw or paint. You can also take **pictures** with a camera. I have a **picture** of a boat on my wall. ▲ **pictures.**

# Directions

## NATURAL DYEING

### WHAT YOU WILL NEED:

- stove or hot plate
- large kettle
- water
- a white cotton garment (T-shirt, socks)
- various natural substances

| NATURAL SUBSTANCES DYE CHART | | | |
|---|---|---|---|
| marigold flowers | | red onion skin | |
| sage | | acorns | |
| walnut shells | | berries | |
| tea | | coffee | |
| spinach | | dandelion roots | |
| yellow onion skin | | beets | |

# Directions

## WHAT TO DO:

1. Fill the large kettle with water and put it on the stove or hot plate.
2. Turn on the heat.
3. Add the natural substance for the color you want.
4. Allow the water to simmer until it is darker than you want your garment to be.
5. Put the garment loosely into the water and simmer it until it is darker than you want it. (The garment will be lighter when it dries.)
6. Remove the garment from the kettle and rinse it in cold water.
7. Wring out the garment and hang it up to dry.
8. If you are not going to dye anything else, turn off the heat and empty the kettle.

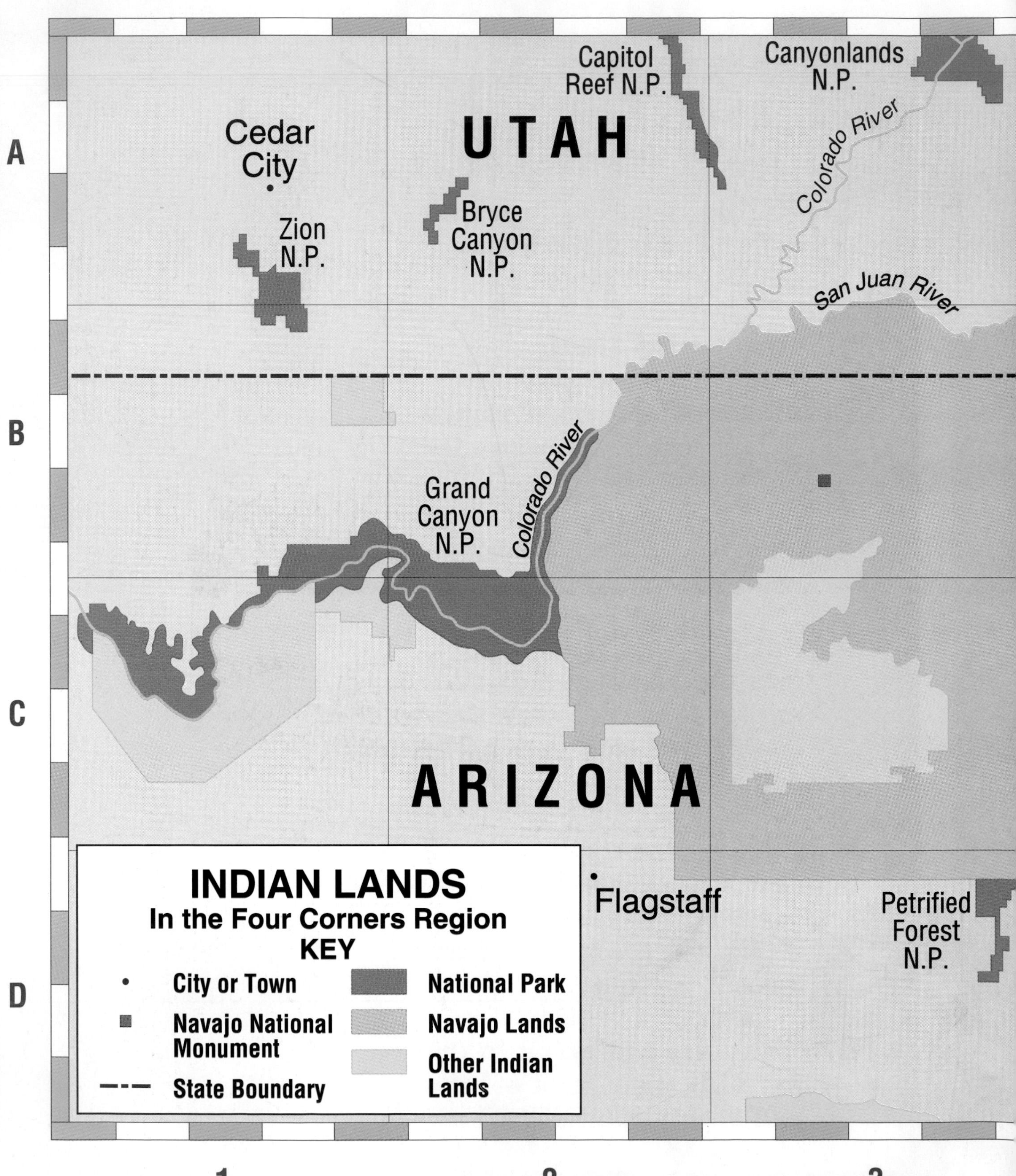
1
2
3
A
B
C
D
Capitol Reef N.P.
Canyonlands N.P.
Cedar City
UTAH
Colorado River
Bryce Canyon N.P.
Zion N.P.
San Juan River
Colorado River
Grand Canyon N.P.
ARIZONA
Flagstaff
Petrified Forest N.P.
INDIAN LANDS
In the Four Corners Region
KEY
City or Town
Navajo National Monument
State Boundary
National Park
Navajo Lands
Other Indian Lands
1
2
3

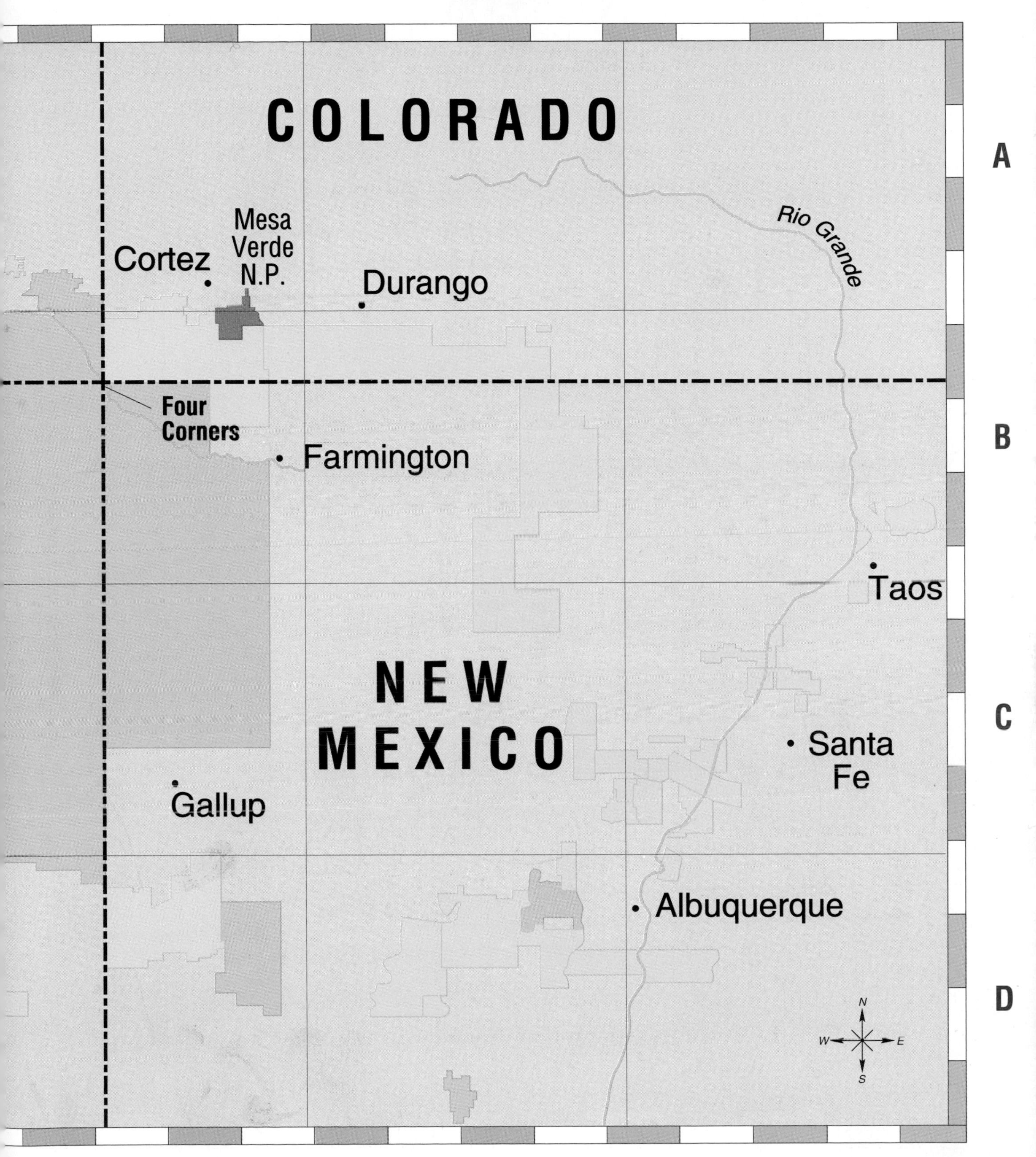
4
5
6
COLORADO
Rio Grande
Mesa
Verde
N.P.
Cortez
Durango
Four
Corners
Farmington
Taos
NEW
MEXICO
Santa
Fe
Gallup
Albuquerque
N
W
E
S
A
B
C
D
4
5
6

# Maps

HUDSON RIVER
THE BRONX
NEW JERSEY
MANHATTAN
QUEENS
1.
2.
3.
GOVERNOR'S ISLAND
Buttermilk Channel
Red Hook
UPPER NEW YORK BAY
BROOKLYN
The Narrows
STATEN ISLAND
VERRAZANO-NARROWS BRIDGE
LOWER NEW YORK BAY
A T L A N

# Maps

LONG ISLAND
TIC OCEAN
N
W
E
S
NEW YORK CITY
KEY
New York City
Water
Park
Airport
Bridge
Tunnel
Places of Interest
1. World Trade Center
2. Battery Park
3. Statue of Liberty

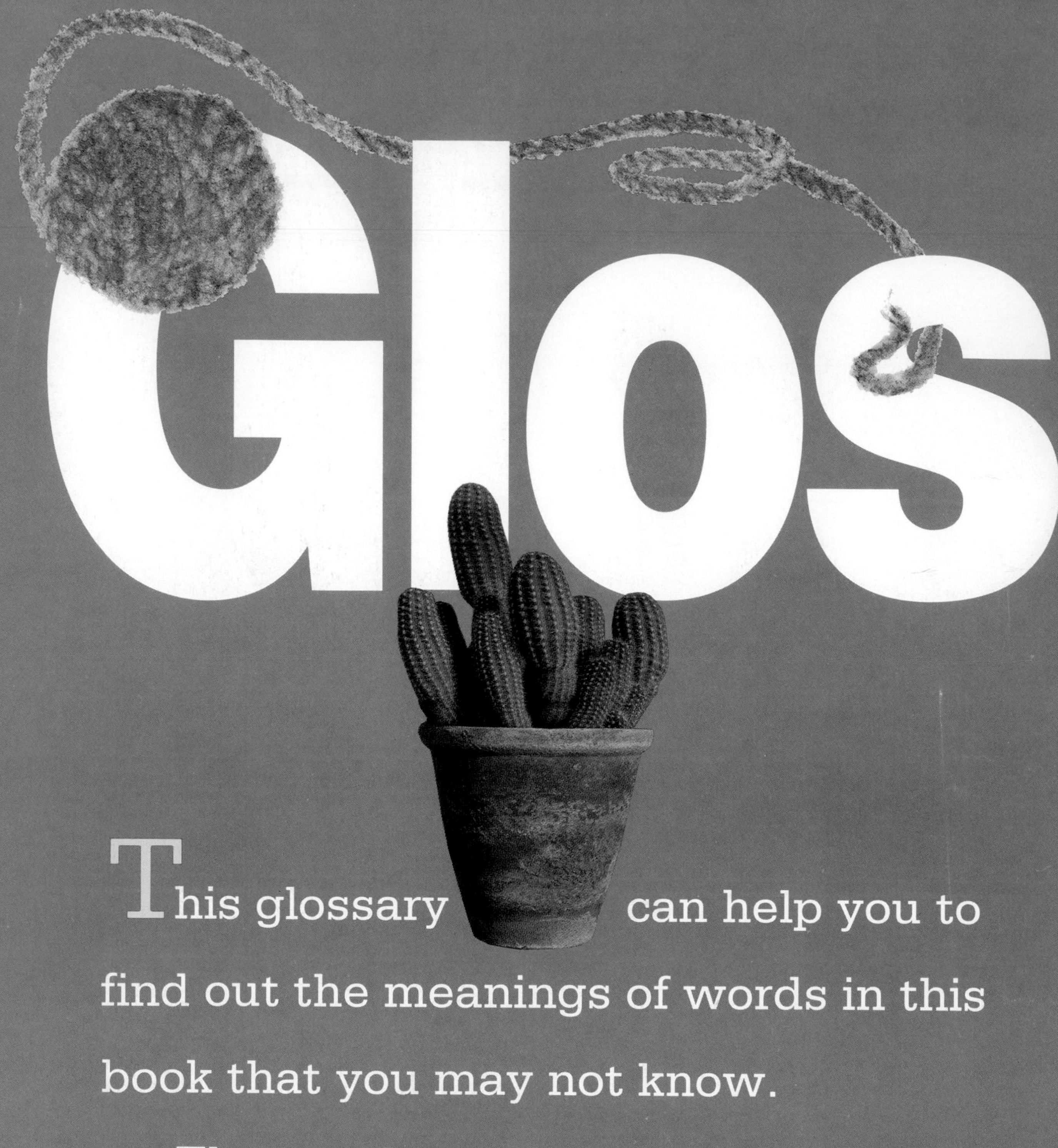


This glossary can help you to find out the meanings of words in this book that you may not know.

The words are in alphabetical order. Guide words tell you the first and last words on the page.

Glossary entries are based on entries in *The Macmillan/McGraw-Hill Primary Dictionary* and *The Macmillan/McGraw-Hill School Dictionary 1.*

**algae**

**Algae** are very simple living things. Most **algae** are plants that have no roots or flowers. We could not swim in the pond because there were too many **algae** in it.

**ancient**

When something is **ancient,** it is very old. Mom found some **ancient** coins in a trunk.

**artisan**

An **artisan** is someone who is very skilled at doing a particular craft. Carpenters, plumbers, and electricians are **artisans. ▲ artisans.**

**balance**

**Balance** means to keep something in a place so that it does not fall off or roll away. The seal at the circus can **balance** a ball on its nose. **▲ balanced, balancing.**

**border**

A **border** is a line where one country or place ends and another begins. The fence marks the **border** between our yard and theirs. ▲ **borders.**

**bristle**

**Bristle** means to have the hairs on the neck or body stand up. The cat **bristled** when it saw the dog. ▲ **bristled, bristling.**

C

### cactus

A **cactus** is a plant that grows in the desert. **Cactuses** have sharp needles or hairs instead of leaves. **Cactuses** grow in many shapes, and some have large, bright flowers. My **cactus** needs just a little water to stay alive and healthy. ▲ **cactuses.**

### collision

A **collision** is a crash. The two bicycle riders had a **collision,** but neither one was hurt. ▲ **collisions.**

### commotion

**Commotion** means a noisy confusion. There was a lot of **commotion** as people rushed to find a seat on the crowded subway. ▲ **commotions.**

### concentrate

**Concentrate** means to pay close attention. We could not **concentrate** on our schoolwork because it was too noisy. ▲ **concentrated, concentrating.**

**constellation**

A **constellation** is a group of stars. A **constellation** often forms a pattern in the sky that looks like a picture. The Big Dipper is part of a **constellation.**

▲ **constellations.**

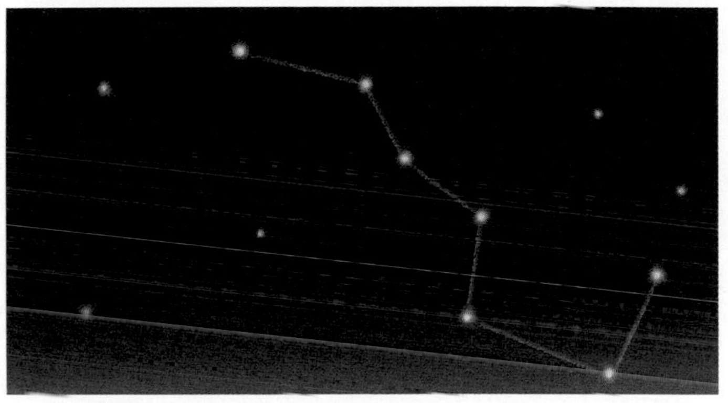

**cornmeal**

**Cornmeal** is corn that is ground up. Mom makes muffins with **cornmeal.**

**cranky**

**Cranky** means when someone is grouchy or in a bad mood. Tom always gets **cranky** when he is tired.

▲ **crankier, crankiest.**

**curly**

**Curly** means having pieces of hair in the shape of little circles. Sally has **curly** hair. ▲ **curlier, curliest.**

D

**dangle**

**Dangle** means to hang or swing loosely. The kite **dangled** by its string from a branch of the tree. ▲ **dangled, dangling.**

**decoration**

**Decoration** is what you do to make something look prettier or more attractive. The **decorations** made the room look beautiful. ▲ **decorations.**

**desert**

A **desert** is a place with very little water. You need to carry water with you when you are in the **desert.** ▲ **deserts.**

### dragon

A **dragon** is a make-believe animal that is big and scary. Some **dragons** have wings and long tails, and some breathe fire. ▲ **dragons.**

### drool

**Drool** means to let saliva, a clear liquid something like water, drip from the mouth. Some dogs are known to **drool.** ▲ **drooled, drooling.**

### duplicate

**Duplicate** means to make an exact copy of something or to do something again. Our tennis team tried to **duplicate** last year's victory. ▲ **duplicated, duplicating.**

**entertainer**

An **entertainer** is someone who sings, dances, or tells jokes for a living. Ken went to a camp that teaches children how to become **entertainers.**

▲ **entertainers.**

**fan**

**1.** A **fan** is something used to make air move for cooling. One kind of **fan** you hold in your hand and wave back and forth. The other kind of **fan** is a machine that moves the air for you. During the heat wave, we used every **fan** in the house.

**2.** A **fan** can also be a person who is interested in or about someone or something. Some football **fans** watch games on television all weekend. ▲ **fans.**

**female**

A **female** is a girl or a woman. Mothers and aunts are **females.** An animal may be a **female,** too. Our cat Joy is a **female.** ▲ **females.**

**fierce**

When something is **fierce,** it is wild and dangerous. A hungry lion is **fierce.**
▲ **fiercer, fiercest.**

**folks**

**Folks** are your family or relatives. My **folks** all get together for a picnic every Fourth of July. ▲ **folks.**

G

**grove**

A **grove** is a group of trees standing together. Orange trees grow in orange **groves.** ▲ **groves.**

**gulp**

**Gulp** means to swallow quickly or in large amounts. José **gulped** a glass of milk and ran out to catch the bus. ▲ **gulped, gulping.**

**handkerchief**

A **handkerchief** is a soft piece of cloth. It is used to wipe the nose or face. I need to carry a **handkerchief** when I have a cold. ▲ **handkerchiefs.**

**hatch**

**Hatch** means to come from an egg. When a chicken is born, we say that it **hatches.** ▲ **hatched, hatching.**

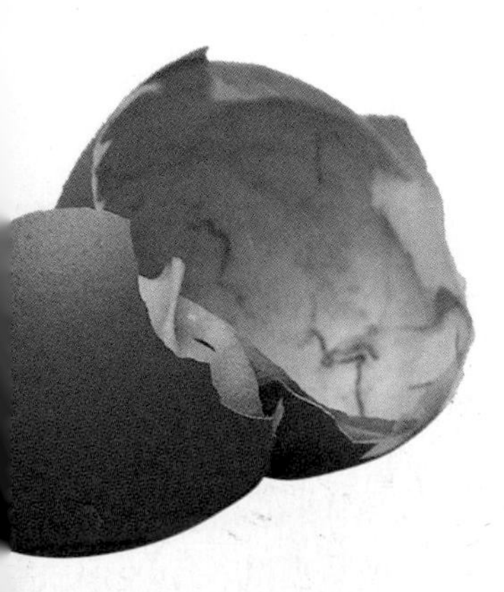

# I

**immediately**

**Immediately** means now. If we do not leave **immediately,** the plane will leave without us.

**invisible**

If something is **invisible,** it cannot be seen. In the story, nobody could see the good fairy because she was **invisible.**

# J

**jockey**

A **jockey** is a person who rides horses in races. ▲**jockeys.**

# K

**khaki**

**Khaki** is a heavy cotton cloth that has a dull, yellowish-brown color. **Khaki** is often used to make uniforms. ▲ **khakis.**

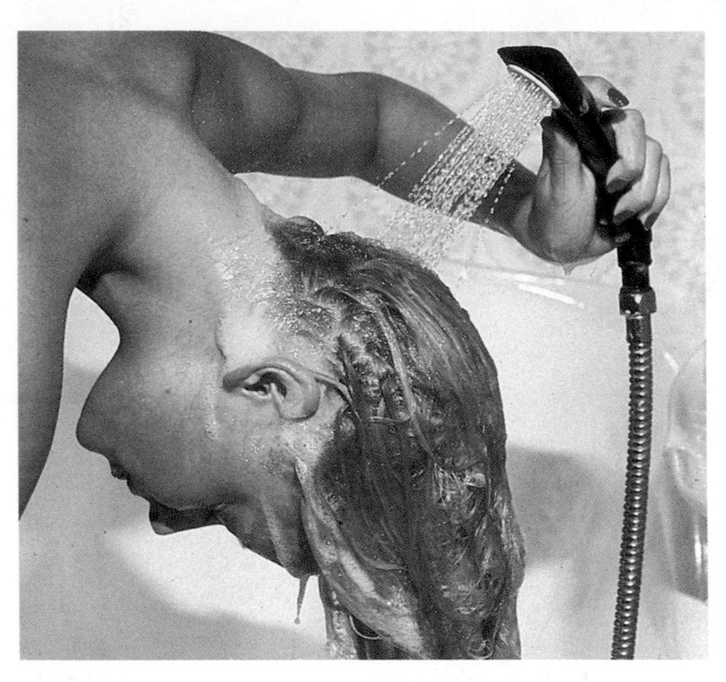

# L

**lather**

**Lather** is foam made by mixing soap and water. This shampoo makes a thick **lather.** ▲ **lathers.**

**lilac**

**Lilac** is a shrub that has clusters of purple, pink, or white flowers. Some **lilacs** have flowers that smell very sweet. I picked a bunch of **lilacs** to give to my teacher. ▲ **lilacs.**

**Loch Ness**

**Loch Ness** is a lake in Scotland where some people believe a large sea monster lives. No one has definitely seen the **Loch Ness** monster.

**marsh**

A **marsh** is low, wet land. Grasses and reeds grow in **marshes**. Frogs and toads live in **marshes. ▲ marshes.**

**Mexico**

**Mexico** is a country in North America, south of the United States. My parents visited **Mexico** last year.

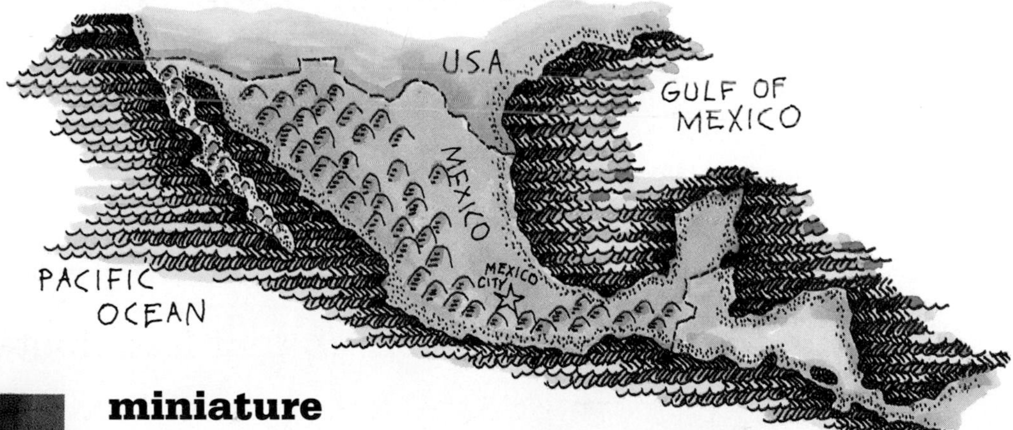

**miniature**

**Miniature** means much smaller than the usual size. My mother made **miniature** furniture for my dollhouse.

N

### nature

**Nature** is everything that is not made by people. Mountains, trees, rivers, and stars are all part of **nature.** People and animals are part of **nature,** but buildings and telephones are not part of **nature.**

### Navajo

A **Navajo** is a member of a group of Native Americans living in the southwestern United States. Some **Navajo** people make beautiful rugs, blankets, and jewelry. ▲ **Navajos.**

O

**overalls**

**Overalls** are loose-fitting pants that usually have a piece that covers the chest, with suspenders attached. Farmers often wear **overalls** when they work.

P

**palm tree**

A **palm tree** is a kind of tree that has large leaves like feathers or fans. It was very shady under the **palm tree.** ▲ **palms.**

**patrol**

**Patrol** means to go through or around an area to guard it or make sure that everything is all right. The mayor promised that extra police cars would **patrol** the neighborhood. ▲ **patrolled, patrolling.**

R

**respectful**

**Respectful** means having or showing consideration or high regard. I am always **respectful** when I talk to my teacher.

**retrieve**

**Retrieve** means to get back. Spike **retrieved** the ball from the pond.

**▲ retrieved, retrieving.**

**reverse**

**Reverse** means the opposite in position or direction. You have to put the car in **reverse** to back up.

S

### scale

**Scales** are hard little pieces of skin that cover fish, snakes, and some other kinds of animals. The cook takes the **scales** off the fish before cooking it. ▲ **scales.**

### Scotland

**Scotland** is a part of the United Kingdom. It is the northern part of the island of Great Britain. My grandparents came from the country of **Scotland.**

### smuggle

**Smuggle** means to take in or carry secretly. The thief tried to **smuggle** the jewels out of the store. ▲ **smuggled, smuggling.**

**snout**

A **snout** is the front part of an animal's head, including the nose, mouth, and jaws. I think a pig's **snout** is cute. Do you? ▲ **snouts.**

**speck**

**Speck** means a very small bit, spot, or mark. Some bird's eggs have **specks** on them. ▲ **specks.**

**stern**

**Stern** means harsh or strict. Mother spoke in a **stern** voice to Buster after he tracked in mud. ▲ **sterner, sternest.**

**streamer**

A **streamer** is a long, narrow flag or strip. We hung paper **streamers** from the ceiling. ▲ **streamers.**

**stuck-up**

When people are **stuck-up,** they act as if they are better than everyone else. No one liked Nancy because she acted so **stuck-up.**

### swamp

A **swamp** is an area of land that is very wet. Special kinds of plants and animals live in **swamps.** ▲ **swamps.**

### swift

**Swift** means moving or able to move very quickly. The rider had a **swift** horse. ▲ **swifter, swiftest.**

T

### taco

A **taco** is a kind of food made out of a cornmeal pancake in which there is a filling, such as cheese, ground beef, or chicken. We had **tacos** for lunch today. ▲ **tacos.**

**tadpole**

A **tadpole** is a very young frog or toad when it still lives underwater and has gills, a tail, and no legs. Our class has five **tadpoles** in our fish tank.

▲ **tadpoles.**

**tease**

When you **tease** people, you bother them or make fun of them. The players on the other team **teased** Kim when she missed the ball. It was mean of them to **tease** her. ▲ **teased, teasing.**

### temperature

The **temperature** of something is a way of measuring how hot or cold it is. The doctor used the thermometer to take my **temperature.** ▲ **temperatures.**

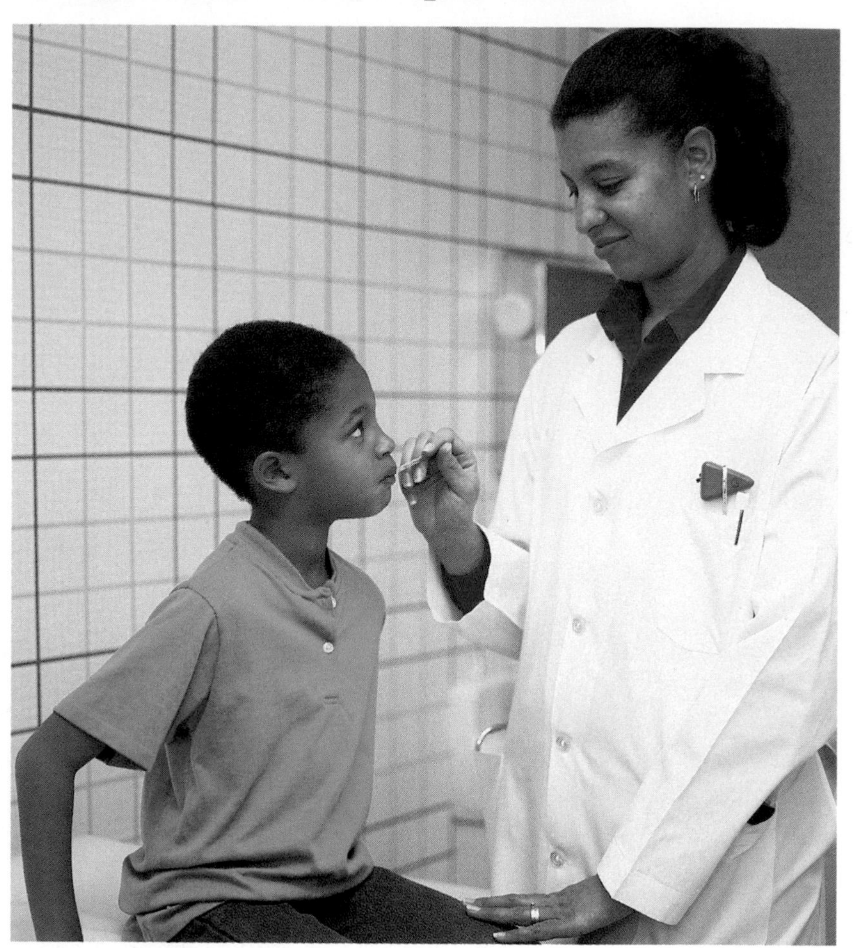

### tornado

A **tornado** is a fierce storm with very strong winds that blow around in a circle. **Tornadoes** can pick up things and drop them many miles away.

▲ **tornadoes.**

**tousle**

**Tousle** means to make untidy or messy. Grandmother always **tousles** Michael's hair whenever she sees him. ▲ **tousled, tousling.**

**treasure**

A **treasure** is money, jewelry, or other things that are of high value. The king and queen hid their **treasure** in a special room. ▲ **treasures.**

**twilight**

**Twilight** is the time just after sunset or just before sunrise, when there is a soft, hazy light. Dad and I like to go fishing at **twilight.**

U

**unusual**

When something is **unusual,** it is not the way we expect it to be. The potato has an **unusual** shape.

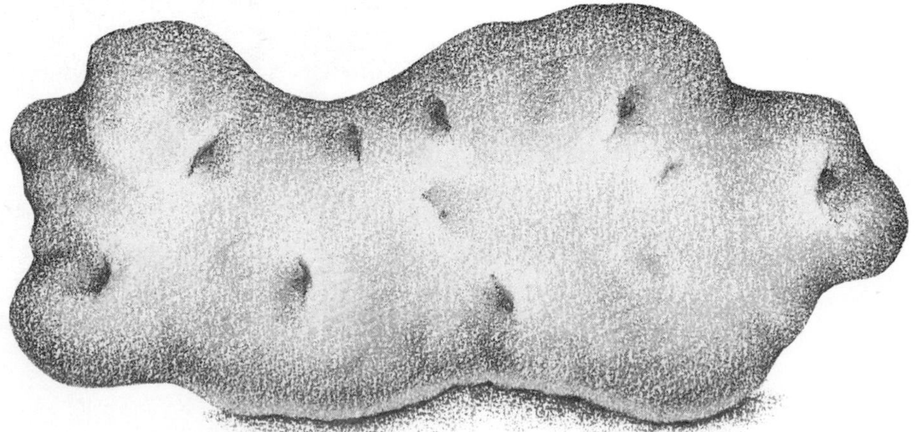

**vague**

**Vague** means something is not clear or definite. We could see only the **vague** outline of the building in the fog.
▲ **vaguer, vaguest.**

**warrior**

A **warrior** is a person who fights in battles.
▲ **warriors.**

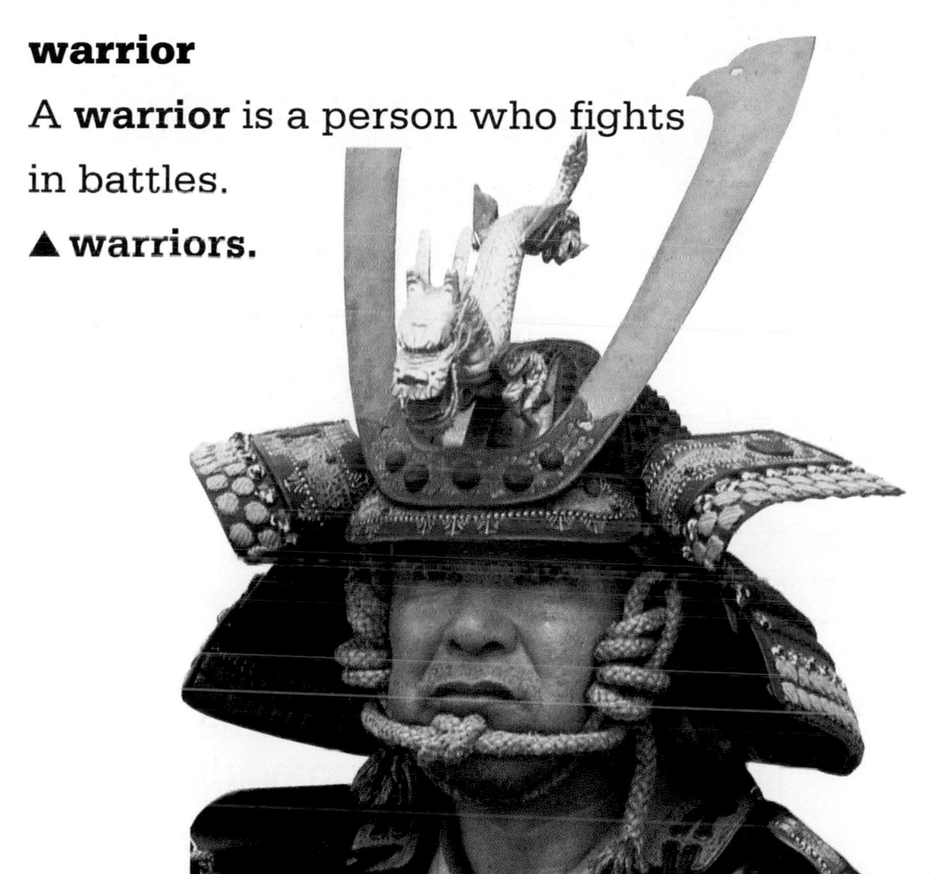

**wilt**

**Wilt** means to become limp or droop. The flowers **wilted** soon after they were cut. ▲ **wilted, wilting.**

**wobble**

**Wobble** means to move from side to side in an unsteady or shaky way. The old chair **wobbled** because the legs were loose. ▲ **wobbled, wobbling.**

Y

**yarn**

**Yarn** is thread spun from fiber that has been twisted into long strands. **Yarn** is used in knitting or weaving. It is made from cotton, wool, silk, nylon, or other fibers. Amy's grandmother is making each of her grandchildren a blanket out of **yarn.** ▲ **yarns.**

**yucca**

A **yucca** is a kind of plant that has long, stiff, pointy leaves and large, white flowers. The **yucca** is the state flower of New Mexico. ▲ **yuccas.**

"My Horse, Fly Like a Bird" from DANCING TEEPEES selected by Virginia Driving Hawk Sneve. Text copyright © 1989 by Virginia Driving Hawk Sneve. All rights reserved. Reprinted by permission of Holiday House.

"The Mysterious Tadpole." From THE MYSTERIOUS TADPOLE by Steven Kellogg. Copyright © by Steven Kellogg. Used by permission of Dial Books for Young Readers, a division of Penguin Books USA Inc.

"Never kiss an Alligator!" from NEVER KISS AN ALLIGATOR! by Colleen Stanley Bare. Copyright © 1989 by Colleen Stanley Bare. Used by permission of Cobblehill Books, an affiliate of Dutton Children's Books, a division of Penguin USA Inc.

"Nine-in-One, Grr! Grr!" told by Blia Xiong and adapted by Cathy Spagnoli. Text copyright © 1989 by Cathy Spagnoli. Illustrations copyright © 1989 by Nancy Hom. Reprinted by permission of GRM Associates, Inc., Agents for Children's Book Press.

"October Saturday" by Bobbi Katz. Copyright © 1990 by Bobbi Katz. Used by permission of Bobbi Katz, who controls all rights.

The book cover of PATRICK'S DINOSAURS by Carol Carrick, illustrated by Donald Carrick, Copyright © 1983, published by Clarion Books of Houghton Mifflin, is reprinted by permission of the publisher.

"Puppy and I" from WHEN WE WERE VERY YOUNG by A. A. Milne. Copyright 1924 by E.P. Dutton. Renewed 1952 by A. A. Milne. Used by permission of Dutton Children's Books, a division of Penguin Books USA Inc.

"Relatives" from THE BUTTERFLY JAR by Jeff Moses. Copyright © 1989 by Jeff Moss. Used by permission of Bantam Books, a division of Bantam Doubleday Dell Publishing Group, Inc.

The book of SLEEP OUT by Carol Carrick, illustrated by Donald Carrick. Copyright © 1979, published by Clarion Books of Houghton Mifflin, is reprinted by permission of the publisher.

"Swimmy." From SWIMMY by Leo Lionni. Copyright © 1963 by Leo Lionni. Reprinted by permission of Pantheon Books, a division of Random House, Inc.

The book cover of THE WALL by Eve Bunting, illustrated by Ronald Himler, Copyright © 1990, published by Houghton Mifflin, is reprinted by permission of the publisher.

"The Wednesday Surprise." From THE WEDNESDAY SURPRISE by Eve Bunting with illustrations by Donald Carrick. Text copyright © 1989 by Eve Bunting. Illustrations copyright © 1989 by Donald Carrick. Reprinted by permission of Clarion Books, a Houghton Mifflin Co. imprint.

"We're all a family under one sky" is from the recording UNDER ONE SKY (Gentle Wind 1012) by Ruth Pelham. Words and music copyright © 1982 Ruth Pelham ASCAP/Ruth Pelham Music Activities: Music Mobile, Inc., P.O. Box 0024, Albany, NY 12000.

"Willie's Not the Hugging Kind' is the entire work from WILLIE'S NOT THE HUGGING KIND by Joyce Durham Barrett, illustrated by Pat Cummings. Text copyright © 1989 by Joyce Durham Barrett. Illustrations copyright © 1989 by Pat Cummings. Reprinted by permission of Harper/Collins Publishers.

"What in the World?" from THERE IS NO RHYME FOR SILVER by Eve Merriam. Copyright © 1962 by Eve Merriam. Copyright renewed by Eve Merriam. Reprinted by permission of Marian Reiner for the author.

**INFORMATION ILLUSTRATED**

Book Parts: Excerpt from HENRY AND MUDGE AND THE BEDTIME THUMPS by Cynthia Rylant, illustrated by Suçie Stevenson. Text, copyright © 1991 by Cynthia Rylant. Illustration, copyright © 1991 by Suçie Stevenson. Reprinted by permission of Bradbury Press, an affiliate of Macmillan, Inc.

Dictionary: Excerpt from MACMILLAN PRIMARY DICTIONARY, copyright © 1991 by Macmillan/McGraw-Hill School Publishing Company. Reprinted by permission of Macmillan/McGraw-Hill School Publishing Company.

**COVER DESIGN:** WYD Design
**COVER ILLUSTRATION:** Ray-Mel Cornelius

**DESIGN CREDITS**
Sheldon Cotler + Associates Editorial Group, *Unit 1, Glossary*
Designframe Incorporated, 66-67, 168-169, 280-281
Notovitz Design Inc., *Information Illustrated*
WYD Design, 118-121

**ILLUSTRATION CREDITS**
**Unit 1:** Edward Parker, 10-13; Mary Collier, 28-29; Jada Rowland, 53; Steve Henry, 88-89; Peggy Tagel, 90-109; Sennelli Ortiz, 110-111. **Unit 2:** Gary Yealdhall, 112-115; Margaret Cusak, 142-143; Jackie Snider, 164-165; Alex Grace, 166-167; Catherine O'Neill, 218-219. **Unit 3:** Mark Bruehner, 220-223; Carol Schwartz, 224-225; Barbara Hoopes Ambler, 306-307; Alex Bloch, 306-307; Loretta Krupinski, 324-325. **Information Illustrated:** Randy Chewning, 328, 329, 332, 333; Alex Bloch, 334, 335; Graphic Chart and Map Co., 336-339. **Glossary:** Dave Maloney, 343; David Uhl, 345; Patrick O. Chapin, 347; Jada Rowland, 348; Andrea Tachiera, 348; Daniel Mark Duffy, 351; George Ulrich, 353; Peggy Tagel, 355; Robin Gourley, 356; Andrea Tachiera, 359, Scott Webber, 361, Carolyn Croll, 363 (t), Neverne Covington, 363 (b); Jean Stephens, 364; Jada Rowland, 366.

**PHOTOGRAPHY CREDITS**
All photographs are by the Macmillan/McGraw-Hill School Division (MMSD) except as noted below.
**Unit 1:** 14: t.l. Margaret Miller; m. Richard Chestnut for MMSD. 53: Courtesy of Vyanne Samuels. 54-55: Photo by Arie de Zanger for MMSD. 56-57: Lynn Sugarman. 87: Courtesy of William Morrow. 90: Joe Samberg. **Unit 2:**116: t. Courtesy of Joyce Durham Barret. 144-162: Colleen Stanley Bare. 163: Baird Photo Service. 189: Courtesy of Blia Xiong. 190: t. Marsha Nordby/Bruce Coleman; b., m.l., m.r. Seny Norasingh. 191: t., m. Seny Norasingh. 190-191: Scott Harvey for MMSD. 216: Courtesy of Eve Bunting. 217: Ned Manter. **Unit 3:** 253: Michael Biondo. 278: m. Courtesy of Martin Link; b. Courtesy of Charles Blood. 279: Jay Carpenter, 280-281: F. Dennis Lessard, courtesy of Chandler Institute, Santa Fe, New Mexico. 282-283: Glenn Wexler. 305: b. Courtesy of Andrea Baruffi. 308: Photo by Massimi Pacifico, courtesy of Knopf.**Glossary:** 340: A. B. Joyce/Photo Researchers. 341: t.l. Bruno J. Zehnder/Peter Arnold, Inc.; r. Carousel, Inc. 342: Carousel, Inc. 343: H. Armstrong Roberts. 344: A. B. Joyce/Photo Researchers. 345: H. Roberts; b. H. Armstrong Roberts. 349: Tim Davis/Photo Researchers, Inc. 350: Tom McHugh/Photo Researchers, Inc. 351: Camerique/H. Armstrong Roberts. 252: t. AEFA/H. Armstrong Roberts; b. G. Aherns/H. Armstrong Roberts. 353: Werner H. Muller/Peter Arnold, Inc. 354: t. Luis C. Marigo/Peter Arnold, Inc.; b. H. Armstrong Roberts. 356: Sybil Shackman/Monkmeyer Press. 357: Prettyman/PhotoEdit. 358: t. Larry Lefever/Grant Heilman Photos; b. Hal Harrison/Grant Heilman Photos. 360: t. Mark Rollo/Photo Researchers, Inc.; b. Tony Freeman/PhotoEdit. 362: Merrit Vincent/PhotoEdit. 364: James H. Karales/Peter Arnold, Inc. 365: Bruno J. Zehnder/Peter Arnold, Inc. 366: Grant Heilman Photos.